A QUIET STRENGTH

Meditations on the Masculine Soul

**Wayne Kritsberg
John Lee
Shepherd Bliss**

Foreword by Thomas Moore

BANTAM BOOKS
NEW YORK · TORONTO · LONDON
SYDNEY · AUCKLAND

I dedicate this book to my two grandfathers, Edward and Oscar; my father, Henry; and my son, Matthew. —W. K.

To the men who quietly pray and use their strength on behalf of the Earth and her inhabitants. —J. L.

For my uncle Dale Lewis Miller; my grandfather, Col. Walter Shepard Bliss, Sr.; and my father, Capt. Walter Shepard Bliss, Jr. —S. B.

A QUIET STRENGTH
A Bantam Book / September 1994

Excerpt from "The Peace of Wild Things" in *Openings*, copyright © 1968 by Wendell Berry, reprinted by permission of Harcourt Brace & Company. *For the Machado piece:* Reprinted from *Times Alone: Selected Poems of Antonio Machado*, chosen and translated by Robert Bly, copyright 1983, Wesleyan U. Press. Reprinted with permission of Robert Bly. *The passage beginning "If I reach my hands down":* Excerpted from "Snowfall in the Afternoon," reprinted from *Silence in the Snowy Fields* by Robert Bly, copyright 1962 by Robert Bly, Wesleyan U. Press. Reprinted with his permission. *The Hesse piece:* Excerpted from "Sometimes" by Hermann Hesse, translated by Robert Bly. Reprinted from *News of the Universe*, Sierra Club Books, 1980, reprinted with permission of Robert Bly. Excerpt from "In the Month of May" in *Loving a Woman in Two Worlds* by Robert Bly, copyright 1985, reprinted by permission of Dial Press.

ISBN 0-553-35121-4

Published simultaneously in the United States and Canada

Bantam Books are published by Bantam Books, a division of Bantam Doubleday Dell Publishing Group, Inc. Its trademark, consisting of the words "Bantam Books" and the portrayal of a rooster, is Registered in U.S. Patent and Trademark Office and in other countries. Marca Registrada. Bantam Books, 1540 Broadway, New York, New York 10036.

Foreword

Every once in a while a man in the audience where I'm speaking will stand up and express his displeasure with me. It turns out I am not the wild, hairy, shadowy, dark, loud, muscled brute he had hoped to see. I've encountered this expectation in other contexts; we sometimes have the mistaken notion that when soul is allowed to reveal itself, the result will be liberation from the restrictions of convention, manners, mildness, and civility. In short, freedom means shadow, defined as unrestraint. From a different point of view, beautiful and liberated human presence is varied and always individual. For example, it is not rare for genuine personal strength to be clothed in gentility and quiet—hence, my appreciation for this book's title.

I also feel uneasy when someone observes my interest in the arts, or my attempts as a writer to show some vulnerability and personal presence, and labels these tastes "feminine." I'm sure men and women in various places live in styles that are specific to gender. Yet I'm concerned about making a philosophy out of this experience. Abstractions and programs about gender always miss the mark, because gender, genuine and full of blood, can never be separated in real life from individuality. Gender and individuality are two sides of a coin, one infusing and shaping the other.

We are still far from a world in which women can be free to live out their individuality and men have abandoned conventional roles that limit their self-expression; yet the way to break out of these shackles is not to set up new restrictive and moralistic conceptions of male and female. Gender will be expressed in the free manifestation of individuality and community. Accordingly, this book presents a wide range of emotion and experience, with a strong emphasis on individual expression, daring us to be persons rather than embodied principles.

As I write now, I think of recent moments of intensely engaged living: a late-night drink with two priests—an evening of stirring "male bonding"; an idyllic afternoon bicycle ride with my wife and daughter through welcoming evergreens and past friendly cows; hopeful but struggling attempts to be a good stepfather to a bright six-year-old boy; days and days of speaking about soul to large gatherings of people of heart. Gender is profoundly involved in all these pleasures, but it is not one thing. The soulful life appears when theories are given blood, when one's individuality and intimations of gender are discovered by allowing life to enter one's tender portals, there to change the mind and affect the heart.

The words of wisdom and the meditations found in this volume can help us stay open to experience. The most difficult thing is not to find new ways to be clever and successful but to get out of the way, create some space for soul to happen, let that long-sought personhood appear in its own time. A thoughtful book like this encourages contemplation rather than hyperactivity, and, oddly, we need good words in order to find fruitful silence.

—Thomas Moore,
author of *Care of the Soul* and *Soul Mates*

Preface

Often a man's day slips through his grasp the way his childhood did—too quickly, without notice. And many of the words we read and hear throughout the day disappear into that place where words go when they do not speak directly to the body and the soul. The thoughts in this book are intended to help you slow down, that you might rediscover the openness that was the blessing of childhood, when each experience had the potential to nurture the soul, when every word that fell into your ears and appeared before your eyes carried great power—and perhaps a little magic.

These meditations were created to touch you and teach you, to help reconnect you in small but significant ways to the universe that gave you birth. Once each day, set aside a little time away from your busy routine to read these messages. Breathe slowly and fully as you do. Honor whatever memories, images, thoughts, feelings, and desires arise. Whether you celebrate this ritual first thing in the morning before the world calls you to disappear into your work, or at midday when you crave a little nourishment, or in the gathering darkness before body and soul settle into sleep, you will quietly renew your strength—strength not just to survive but to *live* more openly, and right out loud.

Some of these words are addressed specifically to male bodies that, for far too long a time, have suffered wounds and carried heavy burdens. Those bodies have been shut down but are now opening and healing, sometimes slowly, sometimes painfully, and oftentimes gracefully. Others of these words speak to the mind, that enchanted loom of thought and perception. Still others speak to the spirit, honoring our masculinity in all its various and beautiful manifestations. We hope that women will also read these essays—to learn more about men, and perhaps to discover elements of the masculine that lie within them as well.

We hope these meditations comfort you, nourish you—and sometimes irritate you just a little, so you will not settle for anything less than the full experience of life that you, as a man, deserve. We trust these words will quietly increase your strength to move into and out of each day a little more fluidly, a lot more slowly, and a great deal more sanely. These meditations are an offering to the growing community of men who are exploring their interior world with the same love and gusto they have given for so long to their exterior world.

A Quiet Strength celebrates the *whole man*—body, mind, and soul.

Wayne Kritsberg
Olympia, Washington

John Lee
Austin, Texas

Shepherd Bliss
Berkeley and Sebastopol, California

1. Being a Man

*Man "becomes" man only by the intelligence,
but he "is" a man only by the heart.*
—Henri-Frédéric Amiel

I am a man. Through my veins flow the memories of holy men, farmers, warriors, and healers. My strength and gentleness are real and wonderfully powerful. I can tenderly hold a child, and I can swing an axe to split logs.

I can love and nurture, protect and provide. Within me is all of the knowledge and wisdom of my forefathers. When I seek the company of other men, I find the pure love of a brother for a brother, a father for a son, and a son for a father. In my friendships with other men, I discover that I am much more than what others can see; my depth goes beyond what can be imagined. My inner power far exceeds my physical ability, for at my center is the energy of love, the power of compassion.

Today I will affirm: I am a man.

2. Many Lives, One Man

JANUARY 2

At least I know who I was when I got up this morning, but I think I must have changed several times since then.

—Lewis Carroll

Inside each man are many different boys. There's the restless adolescent who doesn't yet know what he wants, who rebels against whoever pushes back. There's the younger, hurting boy, like Huck Finn, who'd like to put a river between himself and an abusive parent. Then there's the boy who doesn't feel wounded at all, who has enough energy to chase grizzly bears with Davy Crockett and climb trees until dusk!

Inside every man are many different men. There may be a satisfied man with a trim lawn and a bulging portfolio. A restless wanderer who wishes and wishes, who fills his cup with sparkling water. A know-it-all with an answer for everybody. A fool who loves to pretend he knows nothing. A king who takes responsibility for the whole realm, but who sometimes wishes someone else would take the throne.

And there's a wounded man inside who works daily to heal his wounds. By living more fully in the present, he will not inflict those wounds on future generations.

Today I'll acknowledge the energy and existence of each boy and man inside me. Rather than narrow my soul, I'll expand it to include all the different facets of myself. Then I won't find myself confused by the question, "Who am I?" I'm all.

3. Change

The man who views the world at fifty the same as he did at twenty has wasted thirty years of his life.

—Muhammad Ali

When I look back at my past, I can see how far I have come. Many of the old ideas and painful behaviors are gone. They have been replaced by kinder, more fruitful thoughts and actions. I have learned that one of the worst things I can do to myself is to be rigid, inflexible. Change is the lifeblood of growth. If I accept change as it comes, allowing it to shake me out of my ruts, my life is so much richer.

This does not mean I must change everything, simply for the sake of change. Some of my habits are noble; some of my ideas are correct. I don't need to throw everything out. But I don't need to fill myself with guilt about my errors, either. By gently examining my past, I can discover what to keep and what to let go.

Today I will look at my past as a gold mine of experiences from which I can learn and grow.

4. Gratitude

I thank God with all my heart
for the gifts he has given mankind.
Uncountable are his miracles,
immeasurable his love.
> —Psalm 111 (translated by Stephen Mitchell)

Many things merit our gratitude—breath, the sun, the earth, the moon, and roots. So, too, our brothers, even the ornery ones. Everything wild helps preserve us. Those who teach secrets and share their milk warrant our appreciation. As do the brave ones and the aware ones.

Water, clouds, lakes, rivers, and glaciers deserve gratitude. They all support us, each in its own way. All that streams through our body is worthy of praise—liquids, feelings, memories. The pulse. Throbs. Sleeping snakes and bears. And our eyes, which can perceive all this. The sky that holds all beings, and yet remains within us. Glory be to all.

Today I will give thanks. I will remember the little things for which I am grateful.

5. Spiritual Progress

Spiritual progress comes from changing one's point of view.
> —Pir Vilayat Inayat Khan

For so long, men have been taught to compete fiercely in everything. At times we may even find ourselves approaching our spiritual life as a race. We become compulsive about meditation and prayer. We judge ourselves, and compare our apparent progress to that of others: "This man prays more than I do; that fellow is a better meditator than I am." And so on. Our minds can sometimes take such competition very seriously.

True spiritual progress is only measured by what is happening within us, not by what others do. That competitive, hurried point of view we learned must be changed. When we see other men as spiritual travelers, when we realize we share the same road, then the pressure to be "spiritually faster and better" leaves us. If we persist in adjusting our vision this way, it will go a long way toward freeing us from judgment of ourselves and others.

Today I can change my point of view by becoming more tolerant of myself and my fellow seekers.

6. Anger

Honor your anger.

—Sam Keen

I was angry with my friend:
I told my wrath, my wrath did end.
I was angry with my foe:
I told it not, my wrath did grow.

—William Blake

Each individual and each family deals with anger differently; the cultural differences are also great. Advice about anger is common. The two extremes seem to be those who counsel against anger and its expression, and those who are advocates of expressed anger. A third perspective is that which honors anger and its power, but is also discerning about it. Philosopher Sam Keen describes "discriminating anger" as a gift. Not all are willing to accept such a gift.

Living in this world, it is hard to avoid anger—either our own or that of friends or strangers. The issue becomes how to deal with anger. Some people seem more angry than others, though they are not necessarily the angriest. When a man denies his anger and others perceive it, it is important to deal with it, because it will surely affect what happens. Unexpressed anger can make a situation unsafe. Men seem to need to know how much anger is present in a room in order to feel safe.

How do I feel around anger? Does it frighten me? Am I drawn to it? How do I typically deal with anger? Are my responses adequate? Might I want to develop some new ones?

7. Questions

Questions are the keys that cause the secret doors of the psyche to swing open.
　　　　　　　　—Clarissa Pinkola Estés

We men are often taught that we're supposed to have the answers to life's questions, solutions to all life's problems. In our twenties we reassure ourselves that whatever we don't yet know, we'll surely understand in our thirties. Of course, the thirties come, and we are left hoping the mysteries will be solved by midlife. Sooner or later we realize that the most important questions are still unanswered. At this point we may begin to wonder whether "answers" even exist. Such a moment represents a golden opportunity. We sense it's time to stop pretending we can ever get "answers" and start asking more questions. Simply engaging in the mystery in this way brings us closer to our own center and gives us a better chance of finding the meaning we crave in our lives.

Today I will listen for answers from unexpected sources. This knowledge may come from the earth, from a child, another man, a wife, a lover.

8. Answers

I was gratified to be able to answer promptly, and I did. I said I didn't know.
                                        —Mark Twain

Often we think we have to have an answer to every question we are asked. If we don't know what to say, we may feel less than a man, because we were taught that it is every man's job to have instant solutions. Sometimes we make something up, hoping that no one else will catch on. Or we fall sagely silent, as if we have the answer but just don't feel like saying it. Of course, faking it creates a lot of trouble, but at times that seems better than admitting our lack of knowledge.

But we are beginning to see that we don't have to have all the answers. There is such freedom in this attitude! We understand that the size of our intellectual storehouse has nothing to do with our lovability or our worth.

It is a blessing, a sign of grace, when I can openly admit that "I don't know."

9. From Separation to Serenity

JANUARY 9

From separation I passed into Unity;
All the illusions of life disappeared like a
phantom show.

—Nazir

Being human seems to include the feeling of being separate—from others and even sometimes from the self. When someone leaves us, someone we cared for, the separation often brings back memories of other departures. Perhaps we felt empty. Lonely. Afraid.

As children, many of us were left, even abandoned, emotionally or physically. Now we are adults. We do not need to repeat any behavioral patterns learned in childhood to cope with someone who leaves. We can develop new adult ways of acting.

From our aloneness now, we can begin to find within ourselves the resources to transform that solitary feeling into a feeling of serenity. We begin to feel our internal strength. Instead of turning to any outer substance or behavior, we turn within ourselves to find strength. We build a strength on which we can rely—in this moment and in the future. With this internal strength we can either be serenely solitary or we can connect to others. We are free and we can choose.

I am fine just as I am. I can survive, and even thrive. I am complete. Everything I need is somewhere inside me. With this awareness I can choose to relate to others freely.

10. The False Self

Ring out the false, ring in the true.
—Alfred, Lord Tennyson

As boys we learned that we had to find out who others wanted us to be. Then we were taught we had to become that person in order to get acceptance, appreciation, and love—things we should have gotten just for being ourselves.

We developed the habit of creating a "false self." This self became so convincing that at times even we believed it was real. Afraid to be who we really were, to feel what we felt, to say what we needed to say, and to do what we thought was right, we created a drama and playacted our way through our lives. Our performance, however, was sometimes a painful tragedy that the ones who really loved us could hardly bear to watch.

Now we're ready to bring the play to its end, and let our authentic life begin. We're discovering, ever so slowly, that there are people in the world who will embrace our true Self—as long as we're willing to show it.

Today I give up the drama I created to survive. I trust that I don't have to play two-bit parts, that I can be wholly who I am. When I live my life like this, absorbed in the truth, I hear the inner applause resounding.

11. People-Pleasing

I don't know the key to success, but the key to failure is trying to please everybody.
—Bill Cosby

I've come to accept that I can't live my life to please others. If I did try to live that way, I would drive myself to distraction. When I fall into the old habit of people-pleasing, I look closely to see how I ended up doing it again. I usually find that I'm feeling insecure, uncertain, and afraid. Today I can respond to these feelings differently; seeking approval from others has never comforted me.

The only real measure of personal success is my integrity. When I hold true to what I believe is right, then the opinions of others become less important. I must look *inside myself first*, and not look to others, to decide what I will do. At times I may seek support and guidance from others whom I respect, but their advice or approval will not determine my decisions.

Today I will be true to what I intuitively know. I won't deprive myself of support or feedback, but I won't depend on it either.

12. Crisis and Pain in Relationship

JANUARY 12

Seldom or never does a marriage develop into an individual relationship smoothly and without crises. There is no birth of consciousness without pain.

—Carl G. Jung

Crisis and pain can facilitate growth in relationships. Relationships are like crabs. They have to shed their rigid shells to grow. For days the crab has no protection and feels vulnerable. Conflict can generate growth. Relationships must break out of old, narrow patterns and establish larger ones. Crisis and conflict are the hallmarks of change.

When we experience pain in a relationship, we can focus on the positive context and see the crisis in its larger context. What did we learn from the crisis? How did it evolve into something positive? We can imagine ourselves as sculptors and our pain as the clay. We work the hard clay with our hands, softening it up. It begins to change in response to our movements. Gradually, it takes new shape. The clay, our pain, becomes our new foundation and is transformed into heightened awareness.

Today I will call to mind an intimate relationship, perhaps my deepest. How have I been hurt by it? Where do I feel the pain in my body? How did this pain allow me to grow, or how can I now grow from it?

13. Men as Brothers

All men ever born are my brothers.
—Walt Whitman

"Camerado, I give you my hand!/I give you my love more precious than money," Walt Whitman wrote at a time when brotherhood among men was more common than it is today. Men in nineteenth-century America seemed to enjoy working and playing together more than we do in our more competitive and commercial contemporary society. If we could return to such brotherhood, men would be happier and the world would be a better, safer place in which to live.

You can do something for brotherhood. It may be as simple as picking up the phone and calling another man. You need no clear agenda, no goal; you do not need to know where the conversation will go. For brotherhood to exist, men must go after each other. As we are trained to pursue women, we must actively pursue friendships with men.

Today I will hang in there with my brothers. In the pursuit of male friendship and brotherhood, I must be persistent.

14. A Wordless Language

Nature is one of the languages God speaks.
— Robert Bly

Many men have dabbled in, even mastered, languages. We speak fluent English, manage German "ein bischen," use a peso's worth of Spanish, murmur French when we feel amorous. We understand well the language of commerce, of industry. We're plainspoken about stocks and bonds. We know "car talk." We're conversant in the colorful idioms of sports.

Every language has its proper place and time. And language is fun, even grandly mysterious at times. But for us to know and feel that point at which we and our God become one, we must speak the language of nature from time to time. We listen to God's messages there, in the mountains, forests, lakes, and sky. The message is usually brief, and it's delivered easily, right into body and soul.

Today I'll receive the wind's whispers, the speech of the stream, the valley's still, small voice. If I can be still amidst change as they are, I will become fluent in field, stone, tree, and fire.

15. Hatred

I have decided to stick with love. Hate is too great a burden to bear.
— Martin Luther King, Jr.

Hatred sometimes feels like a fire in the gut that burns with painful intensity. Or it can feel as though something in our soul is frozen and dead. If we allow our minds to run wild with hatred and resentment, those feelings will devour us. Hate can loom so large that nothing else seems to matter. Even when we feel justified in hating, it hurts us much more than it affects the object of our hate. Hate is our anger and rage turned inward, on ourselves.

Instead of harming ourselves further, we can make room to heal the pain that lies beneath our resentments. When we vent our feelings in safe and supportive surroundings, the intensity diminishes. Releasing hatred does not mean that we instantly forgive and forget. It simply means that our own pain can be healed.

Today I will release the soul-sickness of hatred and resentment by surrendering to my emotions and feeling my pain.

16. The True Work

Blessed is he who has found his work; let him ask no other blessedness.

—Thomas Carlyle

The work we do should feed our soul and keep it strong, as good food nourishes the body. Sometimes we work only for money and survival, because it may be that that's all we can do at the moment. But often we work this way because we're living someone else's life rather than our own. Are we working to bring a father's, or a mother's, dreams to fruition? Or perhaps we have convinced ourselves that it's better to be rich than happy. Do we believe the two are mutually exclusive? We must reflect on these questions with courage, to find out whether we're doing work that blesses ourselves and others.

Before the years run out, we need to be sure we're not running from our heart's desire out of fear or a desire for approval. We must be true to our inner life, because it's the only life we can be certain of.

Today I'll look at my work. If it doesn't ring true, if it's not "my bliss," I'll do some interior work necessary to discover my next step. If I find that I'm doing what I'm meant to do, then it falls to me to feel thankful.

17. Self-Worth

Man becomes great exactly in the degree to which he works for the welfare of his fellow man.

—Mahatma Gandhi

My love is my weight.

—Saint Augustine

We men are taught to rely on our productivity, to evaluate our worth according to the size of our bank accounts. In subtle ways, we are taught that we're only as important as our acquisitions. Even in casual conversations, we're indirectly asked how much money we make, by people who hardly even know us: "What kind of car do you drive? Where do you live? Which school does your child attend?" So many questions seek to measure and define us by the "stuff" in our lives.

Our true worth cannot be so measured. A human being is priceless. How we feel about ourselves is what's important. We must allow our internal guidance to reveal our worth to ourselves. This guidance includes our values, the way we express goodwill in the world, and our spiritual commitment to contribute to its betterment. Nothing else is so important.

Today I will look beyond the externals of my life and peer into my soul. It is there that I will experience my own great worth.

18. Silence

Let us be silent, that we may hear the whispers of the Gods.

—Ralph Waldo Emerson

Too much noise. Too much talking. Too much radio and TV. In America today we are literally addicted to noise. "I turn on the TV the minute I return home from work," a man lamented during a recent gathering. "I do not even listen. It dulls my feelings." Contemporary men have become good at shutting off our feelings by turning up the noise. It is time to turn off the noisemakers and turn on our feelings. When we are silent, our feelings can emerge.

How can what Emerson calls "the Gods" (by which he seems to mean guides) compete with such modern technology, which has the cumulative effect of dulling us? These Gods, be they from outer worlds or inner worlds, are not electronic and cannot be amplified. They can be missed in our world today. We need to withdraw from our addiction to TV, to radio, to the Walkman, and listen again to the Gods. The growing noise pollution threatens us all. Silence can be truly golden. Silence can provide a context, an environment within which the self can emerge. In silence we can connect more deeply to others, and the Divine can manifest itself.

Do I have enough silence in my life? If not, how can I enhance the amount and quality of my silence? Is there somewhere I can go? Or a place that I can make for my silence?

19. Friendship

The best mirror is an old friend.
—German proverb

My friends see me in a way that I cannot see myself. Inviting the counsel of a trusted friend is often a wise thing to do. Over the years, my friends' perspective on my decisions has helped me avoid painful mistakes and has given me a fresh point of view that I cannot achieve alone. I do not expect my friends to make my decisions for me, but their love for me and their honest reporting of their feelings and viewpoint gives me comfort that I am not alone in the world. With their support I can move through the uncertainties of life, knowing that I don't have to "perform well" to be loved.

Today I will seek the wisdom and the love of close friends.

20. Seeking the Truth

If you tell the truth, you have infinite power supporting you; but if not, you have infinite power against you.

—Charles Gordon

I'm a man who has told lies and lived lies and listened to the lies of other men. Lying is what I was taught to do. I was told that if it hurts, you put on a smile; if it cuts or bruises you, be a "big boy" and act like you're okay. And if you fail—fake success.

Now I want and need to tell the truth about my hurt, my pain, and my disappointments, and I need contact with other men who are learning to do the same. I also want to learn the truth about a man's special capacity for intimacy, joy, and serenity.

Nothing less than the truth will suffice at this point in my recovery. But I also don't want to turn the truth into a battering ram. I may feel shame and regret for past untruths, but none of these mistakes is who I really am. Not one of them diminishes me as a man. If I begin to shame myself, I can raise a shield, saying, "Stop." If others use the truth brutally against me, I can leave.

Today I honor, search for, and embrace the truth about myself and my masculinity.

21. The Dry Time

The pond is fed from within.
                    —William Lyon Phelps

A pond evaporates in a time of drought, and it takes a long time and a lot of rain to fill it up again. Many of us men feel like dried-up ponds, Saharan deserts, empty wells. In our parched condition, what are we really able to give to others?

When a man has been denied nourishment and nurturing for most of his life, it takes awhile for him to feel moist again, and a very long time to feel filled. Our loved ones need to know that, as we go to men's meetings, to therapy, to support groups and gatherings, we're getting a kind of water our souls have thirsted for for years. We drink it in as though our lives depend on it—and indeed, they do.

Today I'll be patient with my dryness, and with the neediness that sometimes comes from years of waiting for rain. My lips are parched: what can I tell you who love me, who are waiting for me to heal? I can only keep healing, keep waiting, keep trusting that miracles do occur and that all droughts must end.

22. Awakening

Every morning, when we wake up, we have twenty-four brand new hours to live. What a precious gift!

—Thich Nhat Hanh

Awakening occurs throughout the day and one's life. Its forms are numerous. Many of us awaken in the mornings without much awareness, probably between 6 and 8 A.M. Is that when you really want to awaken? Or would you prefer to sleep in? Or would occasionally awakening in the middle of the night serve you?

Growing up is too often a process of falling asleep, whereas it can be a gradual awakening—an ongoing process, rather than a single daily event. While apparently awake, many of us really are half asleep. One of the main tasks in men's work is for men to wake up, to notice what is around us, other men, and ourselves. A good run can help awaken the mind. A beautiful sight can awaken desire. Anger can awaken protection and connection. Parts of us go to sleep, temporarily or sometimes for a long time or even forever, unless we awaken them. There is much that can awaken us—children, art, friends. An awake man is one who can appreciate and enjoy.

How do I awaken—naturally, or am I jarred awake by a loud sound or by another person? How did I get up this morning? Might there be another way tomorrow that would be better for me? I will find my own rhythm of awakening.

23. Purpose

Men activate each other's emotions. When men have some purpose and some depth of meaning that they're dealing with, and they get together in a safe environment, then the feelings will deepen tremendously.

—Michael Meade

What is your purpose in living? Why are you here? Our emotions, once activated, can help guide us to our purpose. Finding purpose involves more than thinking, which can also help. Other men can help us find and clarify what we are to do and who we are to be. Sometimes we can benefit from talking about our purpose, as others listen. Other times we can benefit from listening to others consider their purposes. Developing a life purpose can help in many ways. It is important to live in present time, rather than remaining mired in the past or constantly fantasizing about the future and how things could be.

Having a sense of the direction for your life is essential. Where are you going? What is unfolding for you? Do you sense a pattern in recent years, a pattern that perhaps even stretches back into earlier years? Try to discern what your development has been. Then consider if this is the development you want. If not, what can you do to make changes? What do you want to be doing? Why are you alive?

Today I will complete the sentence, "My life purpose is . . ." I will just say whatever comes to mind. If my thinking gets in the way, I will ask my emotions to help me identify and express my purpose.

24. Freedom and Community

Men are free when they belong to a living, organic, believing community.
—D. H. Lawrence

Freedom and independence are essential to being male. Also key is being related to others—in a family or a community of some kind. The Franciscan friars, one of the first antecedents of today's men's movements, have long been a believing community that has attracted free spirits. Some communities restrict, others free. Freedom and community can be contrary, unless one understands the differences between freedom *from* and freedom *toward*. The deepest freedom includes a commitment to other people, even when they strain our patience.

Community is where the inner and the outer meet, where the internal self can connect with the external self. That great British novelist D. H. Lawrence was a skeptic, yet he was a man of deep belief and faith. He affirmed an inner freedom and an outer freedom. Lawrence understood the value of community.

Are you a part of a community? Does it restrict or enhance your freedom? You may want to consider joining a community. Or working more closely with a community of which you are already a part.

25. Wonder

Men talk about Bible miracles because there is no miracle in their lives. Cease to gnaw that crust. There is ripe fruit over your head.
—Henry David Thoreau

There are miracles all around me. All I have to do is turn my attention to them. Each breath is a miracle, every sound is a wonder. This world abounds with the miracle of life and the grace of God, which is revealed to me if I will only look for it. When I glimpse the wide creation of this universe, I stand in awe. Even to consider my physical anatomy amazes me: how many worlds within worlds are contained within my own body!

It's so easy to get bogged down in the everyday tasks of life and miss the miracles in the world. When I look for miracles, I see their wonder all around me.

Today I appreciate the miracles that have gone unnoticed.

26. Creativity

The human spirit lives on creativity and dies in conformity and routine.
                                                    —Pir Vilayat Inayat Khan

My energy is powerful and creative. Unshackled by conformity and dull comfortable routine, I can create new pathways for my dreams to be fulfilled. Although there is some consolation in what is known and familiar, my spirit yearns for the adventure of the unknown, the unexperienced. In uncharted territory, I stretch my capabilities to their ever-expanding potential.

I don't have to go anywhere to find new territory and adventure. When I turn my attention inward, the great expanse of my inner landscape lies before me, unexplored. Simply by getting quiet and listening to my inner self, I awaken my creativity.

Today I will refresh my creative self by releasing old ways of thinking and opening my mind to new approaches, new ideas.

27. Youth and the Flying Boy

In the woods is perpetual youth.
                    —Ralph Waldo Emerson

Because our society is so youth-oriented, many men want to "stay young." Compounding the problem is the fact that so many of us as boys were made to grow up too fast. It's as though we lost our youth before we ever had it—becoming too responsible and too serious before our time. Yet many fifty- and sixty-year-old men still feel and act like boys regarding relationships, commitment, and direction in life. These men have a lot of Puer (Eternal Youth) in them. This is the "boy in the man's body" syndrome, the Flying Boy.

Of course, there is a big difference between "perpetual" youth and "eternal" youth. The man who knows nature, who loves the ancient places, who often roams the woods and meadows stays perpetually young inside. This doesn't mean he stops making decisions and commitments. Instead, he stays clear about his responsibilities because of the rejuvenating freedom he feels as he moves through the wide world.

Today I'll honor the Flying Boy, the Puer. In this way, I can hold a fresh, youthful outlook, part of which is not caring whether or not I look young.

28. Empowerment

The power of a man . . . is his present means to obtain some future apparent good.
—Thomas Hobbes

Many of us have lived for power, often getting it at a very high cost to ourselves and the people we love. In such cases, we seldom feel empowered by our actions. Nor do we feel able to aid and empower others.

Now more and more of us are striving to discover a new way of being, one that allows us and our sons, daughters, lovers, and friends to feel energized and connected to our Source. We're beginning to see that our play *and* our work are creative acts, not so different from each other. We feel a new love of life, a new conviction that even corporations, factories, offices, and shops can be run in a way that nurtures and supports us all.

Today is a day to explore my understanding of loving empowerment. I will cease vying for power with those around me. Instead I delight in finding and using that divine power inside myself. Today may everything I do and say be aligned with the true Source of all power.

29. Taking Risks

To live a creative life, we must lose our fear of being wrong.

—Joseph Chilton Pearce

"You're wrong." "Don't do it like that!" "Don't you know any better?" As we grew up and heard these and other similar phrases again and again, fear and shame took root in our hearts. Wittingly or unwittingly, we often decided to conform and not "rock the boat." Carrying this fear around inside us limited our willingness to create and to risk.

When we step off the edge of what is known, and enter into the unknown, we risk losing comfort and safety. The man who challenges the norm, following his dreams instead, often risks contempt and public ridicule. The man who expresses his feelings openly risks creating a new image of himself in the eyes of others. Yet without taking such risks, we remain forever static, closed to the great possibilities that await us. By diving into our life creatively, without worry about making a "mistake," we engage in life and experience its magnificent diversity.

Today I will consciously challenge myself. Today I will take a new risk.

30. Feelings

We know too much and feel too little. At least we feel too little of those creative emotions from which a good life springs.

—Bertrand Russell

I have emotions. I can feel all emotions that are available to all human beings. Still, I have often felt cut off from the many feelings available to me. I was taught that it was "unmanly" to express certain emotions, so I tend not to be as aware of sadness, hurt, and disappointment. Even though I may not recognize some of my feelings, I still have them.

It is sometimes difficult to peel away the layers of repression, to just go ahead and feel my feelings. Doing so is a lifelong process. The more I throw off this repression, and express what is inside me, the more I will experience my true self. I am experimenting with a new kind of courage: the courage to let the fear show, to let the tears fall, to heal—and then to move on.

Today I will own my emotions by showing my feelings to another.

31. Animals

O to be self-balanced for contingencies,
To confront night, storms, hunger, ridicule,
*   accidents, rebuffs,*
as the trees and animals do.

—Walt Whitman

Men used to be more connected to animals than most of us are today. We used to see wild animals each day, and hold the gaze. Now we feel separate from and superior to them. The human/animal/plant/mineral connection is stronger in traditional cultures. Native Americans, for example, call on animal guides and animal spirits. Animals can reflect certain qualities to us, such as the freedom of an eagle or the fierceness of a bear.

We have much to learn from animals, from their wildness, diversity, and various modes of dignity. Male birds, for example, with their plumage, have fascinating dances, calls, and ways of attracting females. Looking into my backyard, I see birds, squirrels, and wildcats. I appreciate those contacts and seek more.

What kinds of relationships do you have to animals? When was the last time you looked a wild animal in the eyes? Scanning our childhood memories of animals can be a source of pleasure, enabling us to return to a time when we felt more connected with all of life.

Today I will go out, find an animal, and make contact.

32. Father Wound

Much of my life has been built around avoiding the pain from my father. I have carefully constructed my life around it.
—Men's gathering participant

Our lives are greatly influenced by our wounds—where they come from and how we deal with them. There are vastly different ways of dealing with wounds—ignoring them, passing them on to others, or tending to and mending them. Wounds and modes of coping with them are passed on within families from generation to generation.

For many men, the deepest wounds were delivered by our own fathers. Perhaps they passively ignored us. Or they may have actively hurt us. Young and old men alike are wrestling with issues around their fathers. Men who have become fathers themselves, and even grandfathers, often have leftover business with their own fathers.

But we don't have to live our lives in reaction to our fathers or the ways they might have wounded us. We can take the time, effort, and risk to confront our father wounds. Even if our fathers have died, it is not too late to take a step in healing a father wound. Doing so can help our relationships with other men, enabling us to better solve problems with them directly.

Today I will explore my father wound, asking myself how I have dealt with that wound in the past and how I might better deal with it from this point on.

33. The Ground

FEBRUARY 2

There are hundreds of ways to kneel and kiss the ground.

—Rumi

Happy Groundhog Day! Groundhogs offer humans a gift when they re-emerge from under the ground in the thick of winter, bringing the wisdom of the Earth. Much happens beneath us and the ground that supports us. Soil is full of life—teeming with activity.

When we lose contact with the ground, we lose part of ourselves. Two-footeds are the only ones with erect mobility, a blessing, which can also become a curse, to ourselves and to other life-forms that we endanger with our poor stewardship of the Earth. Our uniquely erect stance can separate us from other creatures and their earthy wisdom. Connecting to the four-footeds can help bring us back down to Earth.

Men used to walk only on the ground, nothing between us and the Earth, except perhaps some leather soles. Now we too often have thick substances between us— asphalt, concrete—that prevent skin-to-soil contact. Many men go for days, years, without touching the Earth with their bare feet. This lack of contact can lead us to damage the Earth, from which humans are becoming increasingly out of touch.

Reach down to the ground, perhaps even into it, turning the soil, getting your hands dirty. Take off your shoes, exposing toes, and walk upon the ground, digging into it. Human/ ground contact can nurture and regenerate life.

34. A New Awareness

Destructiveness is the outcome of an unlived life.

—Erich Fromm

When I am truly conscious, I am most fully alive. It is through my conscious awareness that I experience the world. Without a conscious focus, I react to life mechanically, seeing dimly through a screen of old habits and programming. I move through life like a bulldozer out of control, mowing down others as if they didn't matter, or didn't have feelings. When I lose my conscious center, I treat the earth like a garbage can, unthinkingly destroying its beauty, ungrateful for all it provides.

Today I choose to live a new way. When I stay conscious, I experience majesty in my life. I see the different shades of green in the trees, the particular quality of light in the afternoon. Everything is sharper, clearer, more delicious. I am aware of my effect on the people around me. Through the practice of conscious awareness I make better choices about my behavior. I am empowered to choose to help, rather than hurt.

Today I will practice conscious awareness by looking deeply into what I am doing in my life.

35. Men Cry

I don't trust a man who can't cry.
—General Norman Schwarzkopf

Many men take pride in the fact that they haven't cried since childhood or adolescence. Where does the pain of such men go?

Weeping is a body wisdom that children naturally possess and that men can rediscover. There comes a time when we know our own brokenheartedness, when we know with our whole body that it's time to cleanse the soul. Then we let go our iron grip. We throw off the fear of what others may think, and let our tears flow freely. In our culture, this takes real courage.

Today men become initiated not so much through engaging in ritual and ceremony but by dipping into the well of our own grief. Facing the truth of his feelings ushers a man into the world of men. Besides, after we've had a good cry, we simply feel better. Those who say "crying doesn't do any good" are wrong.

Today I'll dip one cup of grief out of my body and let the ceremony begin.

36. Centering in the Body

Whatever you do, it is only through Him.
Through Him, blood circulates in your body.
He causes your prana (life force) to move.
He digests your food.

—Baba Muktananda

Right now I become aware of my breath. I feel the breath as it moves into my body. I experience the movement of my chest as it expands and fills with air. . . . I feel my body as it relaxes, letting go of the air in my lungs, breathing out. For five cycles, I watch the process of breathing in and out. . . . I become aware of both my breath and my body. The air that fills my lungs is circulating throughout my entire body. I am completely aware of living in my body. Am I relaxed or tense right now? Am I sitting, standing, or lying down? What is my body experiencing right now? For ten cycles of breath, I continue to focus my awareness on breathing and on my body. . . .

I live in my body. In the rush of daily life, I often forget where I live! I become tense and tired without realizing it. My body can become ill without my attention, even sicker when I drive it like a cruel master. By focusing on the breath and on the body during this day, I become aware of how I am really feeling physically. Then I'm able to take care of myself in the most appropriate, loving way.

My body will honor me with wellness if I honor it with my awareness.

37. The Search for a Mentor

Other people can't make you see with their eyes. At best they can encourage you to use your own.

—Aldous Huxley

For many of us, the moment finally arrives when we realize just how long our body and soul have been craving the blessing of an older man other than our father. We need a mentor with a clear eye, who can help us see forgotten parts of ourselves, who doesn't care that we are far from feeling whole. By his clear vision, our mentors return our own sight to us. We begin to value our gifts, parts of ourselves that we thought we had lost. A simple touch from him can calm anxiety, bring meaning out of childhood chaos, and awaken vitality and love in a once-barren heart.

Each one of us needs the blessings of our elders. We must receive what they have to give, so that in turn we can offer blessings to younger men. Wounded, we have wailed at the sky. We have felt as we did that first day when we burst forth at birth. If we keep searching, our teacher will appear.

Today I'll open my heart, where the original teacher resides. I'll be alert for the young man who needs my help and a smile from my eyes —a blessing that says, "I'm glad you were born. Let us gratefully share this life."

38. Self-Esteem

A man falling in his own esteem needs more ground under his feet; to stand again he may need the whole world for a foothold.
—Wendell Berry

So many men try to live up to the expectations and visions of others (as our fathers did) by acquiring land and things, even by "collecting" people! We must finally come to the conclusion that we, in ourselves, are ENOUGH. All those who ever implied or said outright that we weren't enough were wrong. Until that moment of awareness arrives, we will continue to work and worry ourselves to an early grave.

Once we recognize ourselves at our full value as the priceless, irreplaceable men we are, we can begin to let go of our choke-hold on a world that can never confirm our manhood, our inner worth.

Today I'll let go of one thing I've been using to measure my manhood, to validate my existence, to confirm my right to be here.

39. Sexual Passion

Love is but the discovery of ourselves in others, and the delight in the recognition.
—Alexander Smith

My sexual drive and passion are natural and healthy. Without the natural drive for sexual union, our species—indeed most forms of life more complex than the amoeba—would just die out. Sexual passion can be a great source of joy and intimacy in a relationship. Joining my body in love with another's is an experience both sacred and delightful.

It is easy to get caught up in sexual "seriousness" and lose sight of the lightness and pleasure of the sexual embrace. I want to remember that delight is the source of my sexuality.

Today I will celebrate my sexual passion and sexual joy.

40. Be Wild!

FEBRUARY 9

Be careless, reckless! Be a lion, be a pirate.
—Brenda Ueland

Do you remember when you were a boy and had fantasies about who you could be or what you could do? All those fantasies are still somewhere inside you. Many more messages are pounded into us—as boys and as men—to be tame rather than to be wild. Our energies are restrained, restricted, contained, and repressed. Opening to our recklessness and ani*male*ness can be joyous and healthy, and it can connect us to others. Wildness is natural. As the contemporary poet Gary Snyder says, "Practice the wild."

Repressed wildness can emerge inappropriately in the form of violence. If a man acknowledges his natural need to be careless and reckless, to go to excess, and if he exercises that need through play, then he is less likely to experience problems in other arenas. We each can benefit from times and environments—such as open spaces and men's groups—where our wildness can emerge spontaneously. Let the lion within you roar!

If I were to be wild today, in my own fashion, what would it involve? What holds me back? With whom might I share my wildness?

41. Success

In America, the land of the permanent revolution, ulcers and cancer often become, for the men at the top, the contemporary equivalent of the guillotine.

—Ted Morgan

Achieving success in one's line of work can have great personal value, contributing to a fulfilling and comfortable life not just for ourselves and our families, but for others as well. Success pursued at any cost, however, can lead to a one-dimensional life, chronic illness, and even premature death. Everything depends on our approach. Sacrificing our personal lives at the altar of wealth and success is ultimately unfulfilling, so why do men still practice this hopeless religion? Many of us were taught that "success is the measure of a man" ("success" as measured in dollars, that is). In order to get free of this myth, we must expand our vision of success to include many things besides business, money, and power.

Our success can only be measured inwardly, according to our highest principles. We can look at our degree of commitment to family and children. We can measure our success by how we treat our friends, and how we are treated by them. How kindly we live with others in the world is a large measure of our success as men. We know we are successful by the degree of vitality in our relationship with God.

Today I will remember what makes a successful human being.

42. The True Self

Self-reverence, self-knowledge, self-control,
These three alone lead life to sovereign power.
—Alfred, Lord Tennyson

Many of us men lost our "Self" as little boys. Now we often feel there is no longer a great Self in us to which we can still be true. We go looking for that Self in our work, in money, in partners and projects. We seek in other people and things those aspects of ourselves that we long to know. Then through our relationships, through our jobs and our pursuits, we yearn for that completion we sense we are missing. We keep looking outward, falling into the trap of becoming what we think "others" want in us: the "dutiful husband," the "dependable employee," "the good provider." When asked, "What do you really want? What feels true and right for you?" we may not be sure of our answer.

Today I commit to re-creating and rediscovering my True Self. In so doing I affirm my Self. I will trust this wise Self.

43. Dealing with the Inner Enemies

*We meet ourselves time and again in a
thousand disguises on the path of life.*
—Carl G. Jung

I destroy my enemy by making him my friend.
—Abraham Lincoln

Men have been making enemies of other
men for a long time. We can't stand the
guy at work, we despise the boss, the
brother-in-law, the guy in the car in front
of us in traffic. Hatred deals with everyone
in the same way: the spiteful words spoken behind the back, the snide question,
the cold shoulder. We do not listen to our
enemies because we're too busy thinking
of our next cutting remark. Or sometimes
our attack is more subtle. We simply brood
in the other's presence, sending negativity
his way through our chilly silence.

Our "enemies" can be our greatest
teachers if we understand them as the mirrors they are. They point out to us the dark
side of ourselves that we seldom see in the
bathroom mirror, but who peers out
clearly from *their* beady eyes.

*Today I'll look inside for the enemy. Instead of
attacking, I'll befriend that shadowy part of
myself that I used to project onto other men's
faces. I'll face the fact that whatever I see outside myself must first exist in me.*

44. Male Friendships

*Friendship is vowing toward immortality
And does not know the passing away of
beauty.*

—*The Epic of Gilgamesh*

Who is your best male friend? Speak his name out loud. What feelings do you have as you think about him? When was the last time you saw him? What do you imagine him doing right at this moment? What is it about him that you like? How would you like to see your relationship grow? Are you satisfied with it, or would you like changes? What do you share and have in common? How do you differ? Be brave enough to think about what you want and even ask for it.

If you do not have such a male friend, imagine him. What would he be and look like? Perhaps he is a man of a different age or race. What qualities would he possess? What would your relationship be like? What might you do together? How would you support each other?

Now with this real or imaginary best friend, consider how you can strengthen and deepen your connection. Make a plan to see him and do something together. As you consider this, do any fears emerge? Does he remind you of someone? What does closeness with a man mean to you? Does this closeness with a man frighten you? What do you want from this new or old best friend? How might you help each other?

Today I will think about what I want to offer a male friend. What might he need from me? What skills do I possess that I can offer him?

45. Love

I define love thus: The will to extend one's self for the purpose of nurturing one's own or another's spiritual growth.

—M. Scott Peck

Scott Peck describes love as "a strangely circular process." By extending oneself and evolving, the lover literally expands and grows larger. Peck calls love "effortful" and "an activity," rather than a feeling. He says it is not romance, dependency, and self-sacrifice. What do you feel love is and is not?

There are many kinds of love: for the self, other humans, animals, the cosmos itself, and love for what might be called God or Higher Power. There are many definitions of love: from the sentimental to the mystical. Love ranges: from the brilliant to the dark. Love roams: very present one day and far distant the next.

Men love, deeply. We are creatures of great caring, compassion, passion, and love. "Manly love," as Walt Whitman describes it, is unique. Men love not only women and children, but other men. The love of men for each other is often blocked today. We fear such love and its possible implications. Yet when we read ancient literature—such as *Gilgamesh*, the first epic poem written 5,000 years ago—we realize how great the love of men for each other has been. A man's love feeds another man's spiritual growth in deep and powerful ways.

I reflect on love today—what it feels like and who emerges in my mind as I think about love. I will be open to a surprise. What can I do today to express my love—for myself, for another, for nature?

46. Asking for Help

There (is) a basic cry in persons. . . . For some it is: "Help, please help me." Another cry may be "Hold me." Or "Don't go away." Or the cry may say, "Let me alone."
—James Hillman

Asking for help, admitting that we cannot do it all alone and that we need someone else, can be tough. Men are supposed to be self-sufficient, which can create a taboo against asking for help and create fear in men. Men are trained to follow the Lone Ranger and the Marlboro Man, who do not seek assistance.

Men endure much unnecessary suffering because of our difficulties in reaching out to others for help. Men are not supposed to be needy, dependent, or weak. Yet everyone needs help. One reason we are here on earth is to help others —and to ask for help, thus drawing us into connection with others. Being a man does not have to mean always being able to solve every problem. Help can come in many forms, some unexpected—a shoulder to cry on, a friendly check in the mail that helps get us through a difficult time, a stranger's smile in the streets. In order to be helped one has to be open to it. Studies reveal that those who welcome help literally live longer. They also have more fun.

Today I will practice asking for help, perhaps with something small. As I do I will allow myself to feel whatever comes up—perhaps fear, or the pleasure of connection.

47. A Time for Grief

Grief is itself a med'cine.
—William Cowper

Heavy hearts, like heavy clouds in the sky, are best relieved by the letting of water.
—Antoine de Rivarol

I have lost so much in my lifetime. My childhood, my self-esteem, relationships, jobs, friends, dreams, and sometimes hope. Some of my losses, such as the death of parents or friends, are the result of the passage of time. And there were other losses beyond my control: the end of a prized job, the moving away of a childhood friend. I have lost treasured possessions through addiction and self-sabotage.

If I lose something important in my life but do not grieve its passing, I am still clinging to it. My unexperienced grief becomes a deep well of pain inside me. Unless I open my eyes to the tears, I will always carry the pain of these losses. Expressing my deep grief soothes my very soul. My tears wash the pain from my body and my mind.

Today I will explore a loss and allow myself to feel the pain such a loss engendered.

48. Freedom

The soul was never put in the body to stand still.

—John Webster

I am like the leaf that a high wind has blown from its branch. Now free from the tree, I rely on the unseen force of the wind for direction and power. Sometimes the wind lifts me high, to fly among the clouds, and sometimes it tumbles me along the ground. This is the way my Inner Spirit works in my life: unseen, yet guiding me through experiences that will teach me about myself, and my purpose.

The leaf and the wind reflect my masculinity. The leaf is my outer form, seen by the world. The wind is the deep inner force that carries me through life. There is so much more to the movement of a man's life than the activities of the body and the mind.

Today I will let go, inviting the power of my Inner Spirit to guide and nurture me.

49. The Body

*Be strong then, and enter into your own
     body;
there you have a solid place for your feet.
Think about it carefully!*
          —Kabir (translated by Robert Bly)

Your body belongs to you. Enter it; appreciate it. You need to dwell in your body, not in some fantasy of what it might become—if you lost ten pounds or added an inch to your biceps. The body you are in right now is good enough. Sure, you could change it, especially if you love it.

When we explore the body, we become more familiar with it and can accept it. What parts do we like least? What parts do we like most? We can look ourselves over, perhaps while bathing. We need to allow ourselves to have whatever feelings we have. Notice any changes or surprises. It is important for us men to check out our bodies regularly, partly to notice if there is anything that might need medical attention. Ignoring a change does not make it go away. By attending to it, we can learn more about ourselves and take helpful steps.

Kabir ends his lovely poem by saying, "Throw away all thoughts of imaginary things, and stand firm in that which you are." From this firm foundation—the body—we can meet the world, inner and outer.

My body is a gift—however imperfect it may be. I will enjoy it.

50. The Whole Man

They that be whole need not a physician.
—Matthew 9:12

I am complete and whole. When I hold a child in my arms, I express my manhood. When I cry on the shoulder of another man, my tears are a part of my manliness. I am complete, just as I am. I don't need any more of me than I already have. It is not merely "womanly" to be tender and loving; it is manly as well. I am a man, and to love freely is my natural way. It is not just my "feminine side" that loves beauty and great art; it is me, a whole man, enjoying and expressing his life.

I claim the sensitive parts of myself—my birthright as a whole man.

51. Love and Death

The fear of death is the main thing that keeps people from loving.
—Salvador Roquet, M.D.

Two of life's deepest realities—love and death—rather than being contrary, are profoundly related. Love connects us; death disconnects us. Yet death can connect us to life. Both are always present in every moment—the love that brought us into the world and the death that will take us out of the world. They are not enemies; they work together.

Death affects us differently than the *fear* of death. Why love this person if he or she is going to die someday? Or leave? Death and a healthy spiritual relationship to it can enliven one with the knowledge that though we will surely die, today we are alive. The fear of death, however, can impede one from living more fully. That fear needs to be examined and worked with.

Most great poetry and art is about love or death, often about both. Death does not mean only the final departure; it also means change, impermanence, separation, the little deaths that are so numerous. When people leave us, it can feel like death. It can also lead to rebirth, new life, and new love.

Today I will allow myself to reflect on the relationship of love to death and see what emerges for me.

52. Earth, the Great Teacher

Speak to the earth, and it shall teach thee.
—Job 12:8

So many men have been brainwashed into believing that the Earth is not alive, that it possesses no character, no feeling, and that it's merely here to serve the insatiable demands of a greedy few. As we recover from this soul-shattering falsehood, a new depth of experience enters our life: we hear the Earth speak, groan, sigh, and yes, bless us for listening to her cries.

The deeper I delve into the truth of my own body and soul, the deeper the teachings I receive from the Earth. That teaching is never stale, never inappropriate—each one of us will learn something different from the Earth, the first and last Mother and Father to us all.

Today I'll listen to the truth the Earth has to teach.

53. Remembering

We all begin as a bundle of bones lost somewhere in a desert, a dismantled skeleton that lies under the sand. It is our work to recover the parts.
—Clarissa Pinkola Estés

Our minds are treasures, full of rich memories. Humans are gifted with the unusual capacity to store information, events, feelings, smells, sights, and most of what we experience. What we take from the outer world we can retain in the inner world. Some memories are so painful that they go under. Psychic numbing is a protective process in which the worst things that happen to us, especially as children, can be forgotten. Then as we heal, the darkness lessens and we can see back into it. There is so much in our minds, only a part of which we access. We are so much more than what we consciously know or remember. As much remembering as we do, there is more to be done.

Today I will allow myself to remember, permitting dim and forgotten memories to return. I may invite others to join me simply by whispering "remember" in their ears.

54. Joy

This time, like all times, is a very good one if we but know what to do with it.
—Ralph Waldo Emerson

When I am at ease, joy wells up inside me. It is my birthright to be joyful. Looking at a tree, a sunset, or a baby, I feel the joy of life. My joy has no real limits and cannot be contained or repressed for very long. Eventually it will leak out and spill into my life. The joy that I feel today has always been with me, whether or not I recognized it.

I celebrate my manhood by letting my joy spill out into everything I do until my world becomes joy-filled. I have a great appetite and passion for joy. When I share my joy with my brothers, we laugh boisterously, play, hug, and feel our love for each other.

My inner joy is without bounds. It is infinite. The source of my joy is the source of the universe itself.

55. The Intimacy of Silence

*Behold, I do not give lectures or a little
    charity,
When I give I give myself.*

—Walt Whitman

We men often catch a lot of flak about how little we speak. Our lovers tell us we should say more about our feelings. To an extent they're right. But we must also accept that we men have lived in a fairly silent world for centuries, and that the ability to be silent has often saved our lives.

We want to learn to articulate our needs, wounds, and desires, but we won't lose sight of the wonder of wordless conversation. We may love words, but as we grow older we can find increasing value in the shoulder-to-shoulder intimacy that men have shared for so long. If our silent way confuses those we love, we'll try to help them understand it. But we won't give up this kind of intimacy just to make someone else more comfortable. In time, those who wish we talked more may themselves acquire a taste for quiet.

Today I'll enjoy the intimacy of silence, the understanding in the eyes, the support of a touch, the love in the wave of a hand.

56. Present Time

The only aspect of time that is eternal is now.
—A Course in Miracles

Present time is where you are right now. Staying in present time can be difficult. The past pulls—patterns of behaving, memories, ways of being. The future lures —fantasies, possibilities, options. It can be difficult to stay in this moment, with all its limitations. We scurry on our way to the next time and place, rather than being receptive to the fullness of the immediate situation. We are often reminded of other moments and other persons and of who we used to be. We will never be *that* person again; in this moment, we are *this* person. Or we can get lost fantasizing who we could be.

To be fully present in the current moment is to be connected and vital. Technological advances such as cars and telephones make it more difficult for us to stay rooted in the moment. They are always taking us forward and elsewhere— calling us to another time and place. Staying connected to the present moment and the people in that moment can be a great challenge.

To stay in present time, I can ask myself: Where am I? What surrounds me? What do I see? What can I touch? As I settle in, what images come to mind? What am I thinking? Feeling?

57. Learning Patience

Knowing trees, I understand the meaning of patience. Knowing grass, I can appreciate persistence.

—Hal Borland

Men learned how to wait long ago. We waited on our parents to approve of us, to love us as we were, to stop drinking, or just to come home from work and give us their attention. Failing that, we waited until we could leave home. We've waited on promotions that never came. We've waited for answers to our discontent.

We wait, but not patiently. Patience remains a way of being that eludes most of us. Yet we need patience with our healing process, patience with our children. We want to be patient with a spouse who's trying to recover, one day at a time. We need patience with people in general: the slow driver ahead of us, the person with too many items in the "express" checkout. For this kind of patience, we also need our sense of humor back. And most of all, we need to have patience with ourselves, as we learn new ways of relating to and communicating with each other.

Patience is more than a virtue. It's a necessity, if we're ever going to experience serenity that lasts longer than a few minutes.

Today I renew my effort to treat the people I love, and even the people who are strangers to me, with patience and tolerance. I will let them move at their own pace, not mine.

58. Look Within

There is a force within that gives you life—
Seek that.

—Rumi

A man is not complete unless he looks within himself, regularly. Our own inner wisdom and inner teachings are substantial. A man separated from his own inner strength has lost much. Messages come from within, if we would listen. Inner guides, inner teachers, and inner protectors dwell within each of us and wait for us to listen to them. Dreams come from within. Sometimes they carry memories of the past, or insights into the future. They are riddles to be understood, images to guide us.

Contemporary society values the man of action, often at the expense of the man of introspection. It is not enough to look outside and make contact with people and the rest of nature. Reflection can be as valuable as activity. *Being* is as important as *doing*. If action and doing become separated from introspection, reflection, and being, then they lose much of their fullness.

When I look within, what do I see? What messages do I hear? Digging deeper, what do I come upon? What thoughts, feelings, memories are buried within me? How can I access them?

59. Meeting Women as Themselves

One's life has value so long as one attributes value to the life of others, by means of love, friendship, indignation, and compassion.
                                    —Simone de Beauvoir

"Women are too emotional." "Women are the intuitive ones." "Women are gossips." "Women are the only nurturers." These are some of the myths we've been taught about women. When we view women through false notions of "how they should be," we limit our ability to experience their uniqueness, to appreciate their talents. When we embrace stereotypes rather than individuals, we lock real women out of our hearts, depriving ourselves of the experience of true relationships.

Each one of us is unique. Like men, women are individuals who are sometimes creative, sometimes aggressive. Sometimes women are warriors, sometimes peacemakers. They have the same amazing range of potential that men have. When we let go of our habitual concepts about how women are, or should be, we open ourselves to the wonderful experience of truly meeting another human being, a unique and complex individual full of surprises, bearing many gifts.

Today I will consciously let go of my mental stereotypes about women. I will treat each woman I meet as a unique human being.

60. Leaping

In ancient times the poet flew from one world to another, "riding on dragons." . . . Dragon smoke means that a leap has taken place. That leap can be described as a leap from . . . the known part of the mind to the unknown part and back to the known.

—Robert Bly

Leaping, as boys know, is essential. Why walk when you can skip, hop, leap? There are many ways to get from one point to another; leaping is one of the more imaginative ways. Good minds are given to leaping, naturally, until the process is impeded by adults who, threatened by the leaping, want to control it. The capacity to spring up and forward is born into our feet and legs. We can both remain grounded and fly. Leaping is connected to the feeling of joy. Feelings arise in our feet and legs and propel us into the air.

If our leaping has been constricted, we can go beyond those limits and recall times when we did leap. Or go out and watch a frog or other animal that leaps. Or play the leapfrog game where we jump over others. Leaping helps creativity—going from one idea or image to another. It also feels good. Great writers, especially poets, leap. Leaping is freeing. It can help one let go and loosen up. You may end up with some surprises.

Practice leaping. Start slowly. You may want to leap across something. Or up something. Let out a sound as you leap. Leave behind anything that impedes you. As you consider leaping, some fear may arise. Go ahead, leap anyway, even if it makes you feel silly or self-conscious.

61. Images of Manhood

MARCH 1

Warriors and toilers: those seemed, in my boyhood vision, to be the chief destinies for men.
—Scott Russell Sanders

When many of us were growing up, gun-toting cowboys and steely-eyed soldiers were the main role models available. Real men were warriors, ready to die for honor. Our only other models of "real men" were those who worked in factories sixty or seventy hours a week, providing for their families at great personal expense. As young men, we may have tried out these "male" lifestyles. Some of us found little honor in warfare, and felt hollow and empty after working many hours at jobs we didn't like.

Over time we are learning that being a "real man" is something that happens on the inside. Manliness becomes a feeling of conviction, a self-confidence, a deep belief in ourselves that transcends the job we do. It is a state of mind, not an image to be projected to others.

What is most deeply important about being a man is different to each one of us, and may not be evident to others at all. Yet we know when we have slipped away from this inner core of masculine strength: we begin to sense an imbalance. When we live by our own inner standards, we are at peace with the world and with ourselves.

Today I will contemplate what it means to be a man.

62. Aging

In youth we learn; in age we understand.
          —Marie von Ebner-Eschenbach

Becoming an elder is a lifetime process. Elderhood is not a sudden event but a gradual evolution of wisdom and experience. Every day that we are aware of our inner unfolding, we move closer to becoming elders. First, we become the respectful student of our own wise elders. We move forward each day, remembering that we are not only a body. The physical body must obey the law of time. Aging alone will not prepare us for elderhood. To hold the responsibilities of an elder in the community and in our family, we must seize each experience life gives as fuel for our inner search. To be an elder is to achieve spiritual maturity. Such maturity is learned in the least as well as the greatest moment; it is the treasure of a lifetime.

Today I am aware that, with every conscious act, wisdom is accumulated, to be offered to others when the time comes.

63. Personal Ritual

To be able to face our fears, we must remember how to perform ritual. To remember how to perform ritual, we must slow down.
—Malidoma Some

Ahhh! The slow walk around the park. The act of slowly sipping a cup of hot peppermint tea, without doing anything else. Breathing in. Breathing out. Making love with the whole body, forgetting everything else. Giving a child complete attention. Soaking in a hot bath. Taking time off, knowing the world can take care of itself for a while. Writing in a journal. All of this is ritual, and it is greatly rejuvenating.

Many men today are gathering to construct new symbolic, ceremonial rituals that reveal and secure our place within the community. Yet we must also find the *personal* rituals that reward and renew us. Our culture provides few blueprints for self-nurturing ritual, so we must acknowledge our fear of breaking the old restricted code. To live in a new kind of manhood, we must begin to nurture ourselves daily, through personal rituals that offer meaning and power to us alone.

It's a realistic masculinity we seek, one that requires our care. We'll have to go slowly. Hurry and self-love can't coexist.

Today I'll approach each moment with a conscious, deliberately slower pace. As I engage the slow process of creating and participating in deep ritual, I'll enjoy also the small personal rituals that arise from a natural self-love.

64. Conflict

In fact, the conflict itself is creative and perhaps should never be healed.

—Thomas Moore

Very often men seek to remove conflict. At times that's the best move to make. But hoping for an end to all conflict is unrealistic. Conflict is natural; it's part of living in community rather than in isolation.

When conflict arises, I can take it as a great opportunity to practice my skills. I can explore, appreciate, and learn from each circumstance. If someone flirts with my wife, I get to practice handling my jealousy and anger. In a disagreement with a coworker, I can practice seeing a task in a new way. If my teenage son wants to dye his hair purple and put a ring in his nose, I get to practice tolerance and compromise.

No matter how disagreeable on the outside, every conflict has a delicious sweet at its core—a great teaching hidden in its middle. To pray that a conflict will disappear before it has done its work on me will only lead me further into darkness. To meet conflicts with an enthusiastic good nature, to work at each one until I discover its hidden teaching, is to live wisely and fully.

Today I accept the presence of conflict in my life. I have the choice to embrace conflicts, to learn from them, to use them to grow.

65. Clear Thinking

Feelings, and feelings, and feelings. Let me try thinking instead.

—C. S. Lewis

Thinking can be a real pleasure. Though it can also be taken to extremes, some people get on such an anti-intellectual kick that they lose the pleasure and benefits of thinking. Clear thinking is a blessing; it can free the mind of clutter. Reading a good, clear writer, such as C. S. Lewis, can be a liberating experience. Such writers can help us understand what we are thinking and feeling.

Conversation with men who think clearly brings clarity to our own minds. Such men—true philosophers—manage to be in the moment, while at the same time they use language to examine and reflect.

Today I will employ the skills of separating, distinguishing, and differentiating. These are helpful skills that we can value and that can contribute to families and to communities, as well as to ourselves.

66. Feelings

Make some muscle in your head but use the muscle in your heart.

—Amiri Baraka

The ability to think, to plan, to solve problems, is a wonderful gift. There is pleasure in using the mind to create, great satisfaction in laying out a plan to meet a problem or reach a goal.

My heart, however, is where truth and wisdom live. All of the wonderful things I can do with my mind are barren and worthless unless I connect with the feelings, intuition, and love that exist in my heart. When my heart is the captain of my mind, then I am connected and whole.

Today I will listen to my heart and let it guide me.

67. Right Now

The present moment is a powerful goddess.
　　　　　—Johann Wolfgang von Goethe

Many of us spend a lot of time in the past
—thinking about what we should have
done or said, doubting ourselves, savoring
a memory, swimming in regret. At other
times we jump into the future, planning
our next move. In the meantime, life *right
now* is passing by unnoticed.

As our recovery progresses and deep-
ens, we spend less and less time ponder-
ing the things we're powerless to change.
With hindsight we can honor the addictions and defenses as the powerful teachers they were, while still recognizing how
those addictions distorted our reality.
When we put judgment aside, we're available to feel and see what's happening
right now, really see ourselves, our children, our lovers as they are. In this simple
perspective lies freedom.

*Today, here and now, I am present to love and
to be loved.*

68. Father

To this day I can remember my father's voice, singing over me in the stillness of the night.
—Carl G. Jung

Most men still need to work on, work over, or work through their relationship with their father. Even men in their seventies whose fathers passed away long ago sometimes find themselves doing work on their fathers. So we should not feel alone if we have leftover, unprocessed feelings about the first man in our lives. He may not really have been there for us. Many of our fathers were Lone Rangers, off at work. If he was present for you, you have much to celebrate.

Can you remember your father when you were a child? What do you remember? Did he stand over you? Was he there for you? Is he still alive? Are your memories pleasant, or not so pleasant? How well did you know your father? Do you feel he knows you? Is there something you did not receive from your father that you wanted? If so, are there other men who might provide that? You may want to seek them.

Today I will contemplate the work I might still need to do in relationship to my father.

69. Giving Up Isolation

No man is an island.

—John Donne

Many of us have heard Donne's words a thousand times; we say to ourselves, "It's true, but why do I feel so afraid to connect with others? Why do I keep on floating all alone, when I know there are people who want to touch this shore, my soul?"

We might entertain a gentle answer to these questions. We isolated ourselves because we thought it was what we had to do to survive. We won't now shame ourselves by telling ourselves we "should" open up, or lighten up. We'll let someone else get close to us only as fast as feels safe. It takes time to build a bridge, to connect an island to the mainland.

Today I'll let myself grieve the history that set me adrift, apart, alone. The more I heal, the safer I'll feel. I'll trust enough to invite my loved ones ashore.

70. Longing

Tell me for what you yearn and I shall tell you who you are. We are what we reach for.
—James Hillman

A man without want, desire, and longing is missing something. When men follow a path opened by their desire, though not allowing it to control them, they can discover great meaning. Longing can open a path toward the divine and toward one's soul.

Certain people attract us, sometimes for reasons that we do not understand. We are drawn to certain places and ideas. Following our attractions and connecting with that to which we are drawn can be important, as can knowing when not to repeat an addictive pattern. We are each particular, unique, and individual, with our own longings. Our longings have much to do with how we define them. It is a waste of energy to try to deny these longings. They then go under and can control from the unconscious. Better to be aware of them and deal with them directly.

What do I want? What do I desire? Toward what is my longing?

71. Centering

For one human being to love another: that is perhaps the most difficult of all tasks, and the ultimate, the last test and proof, the work for which all other work is but preparation.
—Rainer Maria Rilke

As men we were often taught that the center of our universe is work, that we are only satellites orbiting our occupations. We were told that our country is the focal point of the world, and that we must defend her at all costs. With good intentions our dads showed us that we should focus on our families' external needs: food on the table, clothes on our backs, and a roof over our heads.

Now we men are searching for our *truest* center—the spiritual focal point of our bodies and souls. From this newly discovered center we can still serve our jobs, our country, our families, but we'll do so in ways that our fathers and grandfathers never dreamed possible.

Through time and recovery we learn that it's not a "selfish" act to become Self-worthy. By first giving our attention to what is essential in our own life, more will be accomplished, more will be healed, more will be helped, and less damage will be done.

Today I take a deep breath, and it carries me to the center of my being. It is that center I share with every man, a center of pure love, passion, truth, strength, gentleness, and beauty.

72. The Universal Family

A man is truly ethical only when he obeys the compulsion to help all life which he is able to assist, and shrinks from injuring anything that lives.

—Albert Schweitzer

I belong to the family of humankind. I treat elders as my ideal father and mother, I treat my peers as my brothers and sisters, and I treat those much younger than I as my children. We are all on this journey together, sharing this planet. We eat from the same table, drink the same water, breathe the same air. Our souls are much more alike than they are different, and the separateness I feel is an illusion. We are truly one.

Today I will visit with a member of my extended family, remembering that we're all in this together.

73. Surprise!

"Pass in, pass in," the angels say,
"In to the upper doors,
. . . mount to paradise,
By the stairway of surprise."
—Ralph Waldo Emerson

Surprises await us each day. As much planning as we do, we cannot ever fully control what happens to us. We can reduce surprises, but never fully eliminate them. Attitudes toward surprises vary greatly—some people welcome them, others seek to reduce them. There are many different kinds of surprises—some of them wonderful, others not so thrilling. If we are open to surprises, less guarded and defended, they are more likely to happen. Children love a good surprise, as does the child living within us.

What is the greatest surprise you can remember? Your worst surprise? Your past experiences with surprises will certainly influence your future with them. Try giving up some control today and see what happens to surprise you.

What surprise would most please me today?
What might it be? Who might be involved in
the surprise? What might they do or give me?

74. Listen! Listen!

Listen, listen, listen to my heart sound. . . .
                                    —Ancient song

There is much to hear—from the outside and from the inside: sounds, feelings, messages, intuition, insights. We must tune in, open the ears. Ears can close, editing out certain messages.

The human voice can be so beautiful; a group of men chanting or singing from their hearts and bodies can be incredibly beautiful. At some men's gatherings the men are invited to go to sleep around 10 P.M. and awaken about 2 A.M. for a couple of hours. Those early hours can be a time of a man's deepest contact with his soul—and a good time to connect with brothers. At that time we can lift our voices in song, poems, chant, and in memory of our ancestors.

The early hours of the morning are divine; do not reserve them only for sleeping. Our best thinking, listening, writing, and creating can be done as the new day begins, while it is still dark. During these hours, if we would listen, we can hear things often missed in the bright light of the day, with its call to motion and activity.

I will listen more deeply today—to myself, what I feel, how my body feels. I will also listen to outer messages, taking them in more deeply than usual.

75. The Delight of Sight

Seeing you heals me.
Not seeing you, I feel the walls closing.

—Rumi

Allow yourself to see. Deeply. Outwardly. Inwardly. Look closely today; see more deeply. What do you see? Perhaps you have blinded yourself, like one of those horses whose masters have restricted his vision, wanting him only to be goal-oriented and to move forward in straight lines, unable to see to the side. Look to your side. What do you see? What has been blocked? Peripheral vision can open up more insight.

Open yourself today to see the brilliance—that which glistens and shines. See into open spaces, beneath the darkness. What is the light that surrounds the velvety darkness? Accept the pleasure of sight. What is the first sight you recall? How old were you? Rise above, that you may see more clearly. Sink below, that you may see more clearly. Delight in sight.

Sight can connect us—to other people, to flowers, to the glorious. Children can see deeply, and hold the gaze. If no one is there, the child will not continue looking. The child's fearlessness and innocence allow it to take in the delight. Allow yourself to be awestruck again.

Today I will remember a sight that was so beautiful it threatened to blind me. There need be no limits to my seeing and my loving. I can see it all and love it all.

76. Recovery

Circumstances are the rulers of the weak; they are but the instruments of the wise.
                                        —Samuel Lover

We may be recovering from addiction, childhood trauma, war, or any number of circumstances that wounded our hearts and caused us pain. The recovery from these wounds is important. Without recovery, we are crippled, unable to reach the highest and deepest parts of ourselves. As we seek out ways to heal, we begin by acknowledging that recovery does not happen in isolation—we need support and encouragement from other men and women who are healing their own pain.

But I am not merely the sum of my addictions, my trauma, or my past. These are simply events in my life. In spite of my wounds, I am still a whole man, complete in my maleness. There is nothing about my manhood that needs to "recover." My manhood itself is not in question and never was.

Today I will celebrate my recovery by celebrating my manhood.

77. Stewardship

A wise man will desire no more than he can get justly, use soberly, distribute cheerfully, and leave contentedly.
— Quoted by Benjamin Franklin

The things in my life do not belong to me; they are placed in my care. I have a responsibility to myself and to future generations to maintain this awareness of stewardship, and to act accordingly. I will not squander the resources of the Earth that have been entrusted to me. I will not cripple children by neglecting to care for them and about them. I will look far into the future as I consider my actions, understanding that the way I choose to use my own life affects all those who will follow me on this Earth.

My stewardship is a sacred trust. What I do matters greatly. With the help of other men I can change the wanton destruction of our planet and of our fellow beings. When I give more to life than I take out of it, I receive a deep blessing from my inner spirit. Responsible stewardship means extending my self-love out into the world.

Today I will acknowledge the effect of my choices in the world by exercising stewardship.

78. Focus

You aim at the chopping block . . . not the wood.

—Annie Dillard

Whether we chop wood or not, we can appreciate Dillard's point: most of us tend to focus on the "wood," the apparent problem, rather than what's underneath. If we aim at the wood, it only splinters into a dozen small pieces. (And guess who picks up the pieces!) If we focus only on what we can see and feel in our lives, we miss the point. We make a mess. We get frustrated. We may concern ourselves night and day with increasing our bank balance, without ever directing our concern toward our feelings of dissatisfaction. While trying to communicate with those we love, again and again we may miss the mark.

After we've allowed room for our feelings of failure, fear, and fatigue, we can look underneath each problem to find its hidden truth. As we focus on the end rather than the obstacle we can meet our challenges with a powerful ease.

The truth is always available. If I aim for the depth of things, I can cut straight to the truth.

79. Slowing the Pace

MARCH 19

Nothing can be more useful to a man than a determination not to be hurried.
—Henry David Thoreau

So often in childhood we heard the words, "Hurry up, boy, you're wasting daylight! Let's get a move on!" We heard them and hated them because they made us feel lazy and inferior. Well, we got a move on, all right. We hurried through childhood, wished away adolescence, worked hard, blinked twice—and early adulthood had disappeared! What happened?

What would it be like not to hurry, to take our time, to let things follow their natural course without trying to control it all? What if we steered our ship with just the help of God, wind, and grace instead of sheer willpower? Would things really get done?

Today I'll see. Today I'll feel. Today I won't be in such a hurry when hugging someone hello or goodbye. I'll take my time shaving, I'll taste the food I eat, slow down my storytelling. If I slow down, maybe I'll hear the voice of inspiration that is often drowned out by all this activity. If I'm kind to myself, today I can experience rest even while I work.

80. Truth

Truth, for any man, is that which makes him a man.

—Antoine de Saint-Exupéry

Many times I have looked for truth only to have it slip away from me. Even when I try to hear the truth in the words of others, and to see the truth in the actions and forces in the world around me, I am sometimes deceived. Sometimes I hear what I think to be the truth in a situation; upon closer investigation I find it is not the truth at all, but a lie concealed by illusion.

I have learned that the truth is most easily seen with my heart. Truth is more than a collection of facts, more than a logical outcome in a sequence of events. Truth is the ultimate foundation of our lives. Every heartfelt action supports the truth.

To find what is real and true, I search my own heart.

81. Change

MARCH 21

*As my eyes
search
the prairie
I feel the summer
in the spring*

—Chippewa song

In the stillness of my heart there is a sense of impending change. There is a stirring, a restlessness, that orbits the quiet center of my being. I know that I am complete just the way I am, but I also know that the movement toward transformation is an integral part of this completeness. Each day, new possibilities are constantly opening up for me to explore. My concepts of men, masculinity, fatherhood, and all humanity are undergoing subtle changes all the time. My understanding expands and grows along with my willingness to accept myself.

Today is a treasure made up of changes that I will experience consciously.

82. Inner Child

Give a little love to a child, and you get a great deal back.

—John Ruskin

There is a child who lives within me, one of the Lost Boys of Peter Pan's tribe. This wonderful little boy will never grow up, will never lose his sense of wonder and enthusiasm for life. He is always ready for a new game, a new adventure, a new challenge. He faces the world with a fresh courage, an alert awareness. He lives within myths and fairy tales. He travels a road that has no beginning and no end. When I take the time to look through his eyes, I see a new and exciting world.

Today, even if only for a few moments, I will shed my adulthood. I'll be a pirate, an explorer, a hero. Or I'll just take time to lie on the ground and look at the sky.

83. Inner Strength

Perhaps I am stronger than I think.
—Thomas Merton

I often fool myself into thinking "I can't do this" because I have never fully realized how strong I really am. It is mostly my negative imagination that tells me "no" and stops me from accepting new challenges. I accept that my physical strength has its limits; muscle and stamina can only get me so far. But my inner strength is limitless. I call on it when I need to persevere in the face of fear and self-doubt. My inner strength holds me true to my values, even at times when bending to compromise would seem an easier, softer way.

Inner strength is available to all of us. Some of us find our inner power through a relationship with a personal God, and some will discover their strength in the great forces of nature. For others, a life of service reveals their hidden resources. There are many pathways to inner strength; all that is needed is to seek such a path sincerely. When we do, that power will reveal itself.

Today I will seek to recognize my inner power.

84. Brotherhood

Brotherhood enables men to see a bit of their own masculine identity in every male they experience.

—Fred Gustafson

Men today are hungry for brotherly contact with other men, partly because we are so often deprived of it. Such contact used to be commonplace. With the rise of industrialism and the accompanying competition and rivalry among men, many of the bonds that connect men have eroded. The concept of brotherhood remains strong, but its reality is weak. Though there is much talk of brotherhood, there is less authentic brotherhood.

Brotherhood is not always easy. Having brothers means being held accountable and holding others accountable. It includes being responsible and following through and being able to hold things in confidence. Brotherhood can bring many things—pain, as well as joy and growth. Some men who were younger brothers typically have trouble with older men, who may remind them of their brothers. Older brothers may tend to take charge and be bossy. These difficulties can be worked on and resolved, especially in the context of a support group.

Today I will call a friend who might be in trouble and comfort him. If I need comfort, I will call a male friend and ask for help, or perhaps just ask to spend some time together.

85. Giving Up Stress

As long as we have some definite idea about or some hope in the future, we cannot really be serious with the moment that exists right now.
—Shunryu Suzuki

Some of us believe that our stress levels are a measure of our importance. We are so used to stress that a day without it feels strangely incomplete. Rather than feel incomplete, we sometimes create a little tension, a bit of worry, just to liven things up. Yet the more stress we allow into our lives, the more we make a mess of things, and the more time we squander in cleaning up.

While life can't be totally stress-free, we can discover new ways to reduce it. We can learn to run awhile in the afternoon, to laugh at ourselves when we find we're chasing our own tails, to fetch a carrot instead of a candy bar. We can learn to roll over and go back to sleep on an off day, instead of pushing ourselves to run faster and faster.

Today I'll seek out ways to reduce the stress in my life.

86. Blessings

My fiftieth year had come and gone.
I sat, a solitary man . . .
My body for a moment blazed . . .
It seemed, so great my happiness,
That I was blessed, and could bless.
—William Butler Yeats

An older man's key functions in society include giving blessings, to his sons and to other younger men and women. When an older man fails in this vital regenerating task, his sons and others suffer. When older men as a group fail in this function, the society as a whole suffers. Blessings heal and make whole, helping younger men "get it together." Men of all ages can benefit from giving and receiving blessings. When a man is seen, valued, praised, and rewarded, he can develop his talents and abilities.

Blessings can help stabilize, center, and guide. They encourage growth, confidence, and creativity. They need not be complex; the simplest blessing will do. Giving blessings can be mutually beneficial—to those receiving and to those delivering. The blessed man shines.

Today I will be open to an older man's blessing; I will hear what is offered. And I will seek an opportunity to bestow a blessing on a younger man.

87. Acceptance

Nothing so needs reforming as other people's habits.

—Mark Twain

When I focus on what others are doing, I often slip into intolerant, judgmental thinking. This generally leads me to the mistaken idea that if I fix other people's "bad habits," I myself will feel better. Of course, this notion breaks down under scrutiny. No one else has the power to create or destroy my happiness. I make my own experience of life according to what I think about. If I concentrate on the failings of others, I'm sure to be miserable.

It is myself whom I need to reform, not other people. If I am not happy and content, the reason can most often be found in my own behavior and attitude. Life presents me with pleasure and success, mishap and injury—but it's how I greet these events that determines my experience.

Today I will look patiently within myself, to see what I can do to change the habits that cause me trouble and discontent.

88. Seeking Nurturance

Nurturance is felt as a spiritual experience, when for a few moments the feeling of separateness between ourselves and another dissolves, and we feel that we are both the caretaker and the one being cared for.

—Anonymous

Many men think of nurturance only as a kind of care given by parents to children, especially to babies. A lot of us received scant nurturing after about our eighth birthday. These days, though, we're coming to see nurturance as a wondrously subtle form of communication, a fine art, and an essential part of our attitude toward all life.

There are so many different ways that we can experience nurturance. Gazing at the ocean, a deep peace fills our mind and body, and our breathing seems to echo the movement of the waves. Hiking deep into the woods we feel protected, sheltered by the towering evergreens. In close friendships we find nurturance through hugs and intimate sharings. In committed partnership, through sexual union—all relationships founded in love involve an element of nurturance, of tender care and support. To extend ourselves to another, we must set aside our own interests and concerns, placing ourselves in another's perspective, approaching understanding as an act of utmost respect.

To accept nurturance, I must be willing to be vulnerable.

89. Who Cares?

MARCH 29

Teach us to care and not to care
Teach us to sit still.

—T. S. Eliot

So many of us learned an unworkable way of living, a dog-eat-dog approach that causes us to bounce from one extreme to the other, engaged in surviving the latest crisis. I've done all kinds of things in the name of survival: taken care of everybody else, knocked myself out to prove I was "worthy" of love. I was losing myself in the process.

Or I'd try the flip side for a while. I'd pretend I didn't need anybody and that I only cared about old Number One, when secretly I feared that no one else cared about me.

These old tactics failed. In the end, I've had to begin learning the difference between "caretaking"—giving up my own needs in favor of others' needs—and *caring for* people—loving them while respecting their right to live in their own way. I've learned, too, that sometimes "no" is the most loving word that I can say.

Today I'll make a simple commitment: to be who I am. I'll get still enough inside so that I can feel at peace. Before I can understand true caring, I must take very good care of myself.

90. Retrieving Dreams

Imagination is more important than knowledge.

—Albert Einstein

If we believe that our dream life is at least as important as our waking life, what wonders might occur? Intuition is as real and dependable as anything that can be scientifically observed. We know from experience that we become what we imagine. We don't just burst forth as we are, full-blown, without a clue. We may not be able to prove or quantify this knowledge, but we do possess it.

Men can make dreaming, hunches, and musings important again if we try. After all, we were pretty good at it when we were children. We haven't lost the ability to wonder; we've just let it get rusty. Daily, we used to dream ourselves into giants, kings, unheard-of creatures, magicians, rock stars, astronauts. We always intuitively knew where the treasure was buried and exactly what steps we had to take to retrieve it. We have this knowledge still, if we will use it.

Today I'll take time to dream. I'll sail into waters filled with pirates and piranhas—intellect, logic, and reason. I'll retrieve my dreams and present them as a gift to myself in the waking world.

91. Authentic Love

Authentic love is a dance with three movements: solo, counterpoint, and coming together; it embraces solitude, conflict, and intimacy.

—Sam Keen

Adult love can never be all happy merger. True adult intimacy requires some space and distance, some times of differing and conflict. Intimacy and distance are not necessarily contrary; they can feed and help preserve each other.

Thinking of love as a dance can be helpful. We can dance alone or with someone else, in dramatic tension. Sam Keen identifies three movements in this dance:

Solo/solitude: Imagine a man alone, before approaching his mate, or after. He may be preparing or he may be remembering. Or he is creatively pursuing a task or an art form unrelated to his partner. He is quite content.

Counterpoint/conflict: Imagine a couple having a heated argument; their voices are agitated. They are very engaged with each other.

Coming together/intimacy: Imagine a gentle bedroom scene in which a man and his wife settle in for the evening, a fire to warm them.

Each of these scenes has a lot of life in it. An adult relationship requires all these elements for its choreography to be complete.

What aspects of love might I be missing? What can I do to integrate these aspects into my life?

92. The Fool

Turning tragedy into grace is the greatest gift of the fool. The fool may teach detachment but it is detachment rooted in passion and love.
—Peggy V. Beck

Appearing foolish concerns many men. It can be an embarrassment and feel worse than death. The fear of appearing foolish can restrain a man from acting on his feelings. Yet fools can be very wise. The fools in Shakespeare's plays keep us connected to the action. They help us endure when the going gets tough. The fool shows his sad face, then gracefully transforms it with laughter. Such a fool bears the gift of life, even in the face of death.

Many traditional cultures honor the fool as an integral part of their rituals. In the dances of the Jemez people in northern New Mexico, the black and white painted fools connect us to the sacred. They dance wildly about and interact with others. Fools take us to a place beyond rationality. They represent light in the face of darkness and heaviness, laughter in the midst of tragedy, which they magically transform into grace. A fool can lift the feeling in one's body. He can ignite passion with his cleverness. When we are in love, we often feel foolish, and in fact do foolish things that we would never do when not in that state. Fools exist not only to entertain children, but also to bring their peculiar wisdom to adults.

Today I will enjoy any fools in my life—my friends, entertainers, even myself—who delight with their sense of abandon. I will honor the fool inside myself and make friends with him.

93. Breath, Breathing, and the Wind

Breathing in, I calm my body.
Breathing out, I smile.
Dwelling in the present moment,
I know this is a wonderful moment!
—Thich Nhat Hanh

Many of the great religious traditions, such as Buddhism, emphasize breath as a source of growth and enlightenment. Breath is the beginning, a sign of creation. We are dependent upon our breath. Some people still breathe deeply, especially those who live in the mountains. But too many modern men breathe shallowly; we need to relearn how to breathe. Physical exercises such as yoga can help.

Breath is the brother of wind, relating us to nature, of which we are an integral part. The wind has many secrets that it can share with men. The wind has seen much and experienced much, developing a special wisdom. Wind has great power and can transform things—cleaning trees of dead wood and stirring things up, enlivening that which has become stagnant.

Without breath there is no life. Breath opens us. When our breath gets clogged, our thinking, feeling, and being get clogged. It is important to keep a clear and deep channel for the breath. The breath can lead to the Deep Masculine.

Today I will bring attention to my breath. Is it regular? Do I feel that I am getting enough air? Are there parts of my body that seem to need more? I will breathe to those parts, bringing rich air to them.

94. Identifying Feelings

The emotions may be endless. The more we express them, the more we have to express.
—E. M. Forster

Many men have spent most of their lives ignoring their feelings. Today we know that if we cut ourselves off from our emotions, we miss a big part of who we are. We know that having emotions is natural, and that not having emotional experiences is unnatural. For some, the problem has sometimes been that we don't recognize the feelings we experience. There is a wide range of feelings available to us, if we stop to notice them.

In your meditations over the next three days, consider exploring different feeling states. The fifteen feeling states included in these exercises are only a small part of the vast range of emotions that exist. If you're not completely sure what some of these feelings mean (this isn't as unusual as you might think), look them up in the dictionary.

Today I can explore five feeling states by completing these open-ended sentences:

1. *I feel happy when* . . .
2. *I feel sad when* . . .
3. *I feel angry when* . . .
4. *I feel hurt when* . . .
5. *I feel loving when* . . .

95. Feelings

The most exhausting thing in life is being insincere.
        —Anne Morrow Lindbergh

Emotions are neutral; they are states of being that I experience. Anger is not "bad"; it is a feeling state. Happiness is not "good"; it is a feeling state. What I *do* with my feeling states is what makes them healthy or destructive. If I deny feelings, then I repress them and hurt myself. If I act out my feelings by hurting myself or someone else, then they become destructive.

Sometimes I have a difficult time even identifying my feelings, so learning to express my feelings in constructive ways is also a challenge. It is possible, though. The first step is to know just what it is I'm feeling.

At different times during the day I can identify five feeling states by completing these open-ended sentences:

    1. I feel blissful when . . .
    2. I feel jealous when . . .
    3. I feel rage when . . .
    4. I feel rapture when . . .
    5. I feel delighted when . . .

96. Feelings

A permanent state of transition is man's most noble condition.

—Juan Ramón Jiménez

Emotions move through us as a flowing river moves through the land. Sometimes our emotions are fierce and explosive, sometimes quiet and peaceful. We can experience many different feelings in a short period of time. While driving, another car may suddenly cut in front of us. Our first emotional response is fear, which quickly turns to anger. Then we feel grateful that there wasn't an accident. All of these emotional experiences pass through us in mere seconds!

No matter what we are feeling, sooner or later a different feeling will arise. It is important to remember this, especially when we're in the grip of some powerful emotion. At these times, it can seem like we'll feel that way forever. But we don't, of course; eventually we change inside. It doesn't matter whether we're feeling great joy or deep sorrow—the rule of change is always operating. Even as the tears are falling, our sadness is transforming itself into some other emotion.

Maintaining my awareness of the changeability of feelings, today I will explore the five emotions below by completing these open-ended sentences:

> *1. I feel exhilarated when . . .*
> *2. I feel afraid when . . .*
> *3. I feel tender when . . .*
> *4. I feel desperate when . . .*
> *5. I feel peaceful when . . .*

97. Dance

Never shall I forget watching the dancers, the men with the fox-skin, swaying down from their buttocks, file out of San Geronimo.
—D. H. Lawrence

Men have danced together for centuries, often in ceremonies. The Roman god of war, Mars, known to the Greeks as Ares, is also the god of the dance. Men and women dancing together is relatively new. Many of the folk dances of traditional cultures have groups of men dancing with each other. But in our culture, same-gender dancing is awkward. Perhaps if we men danced in each other's company more, expressing ourselves through our physicality, it would reduce the urge to go into war.

Through movement we can enter an ecstasy that takes us to another world. Many diverse feelings can be expressed through movement, including elation and sadness. Men are often self-conscious, even embarrassed, about their bodies. In movement these feelings can transform into genuine joy.

I will dance today, perhaps alone. I will move about, directed by an internal source. I can do so with or without music. I may feel awkward, joyous, sad, strong, whatever. I accept the feelings that emerge.

98. Rediscovering Passion

Without passion man is a mere latent force and possibility, like the flint which awaits the shock of the iron before it can give forth its spark.
—Henri-Frédéric Amiel

As men, we've learned well how to think. We've honed our reasoning to a sharp point. But what about our passion? True, we may carry a passion for our lovers, or for increased income. Yet for many of us, any passion beyond these is far away, expertly hidden. We occasionally dream of "following our bliss," but our actions suggest that more often we follow our bank books.

Many of us were taught to ignore our dreams and deny our passions, just as we were supposed to deny the feelings of sadness and grief in our bodies. We were taught to ignore the body itself, the house of our passions.

But our passions must not be brushed aside in favor of rational thinking. Reason is fine, but even a debate is sour if it isn't passionate. Our passion, not our thoughts alone, gives salt to our lives. Passion makes youth survivable and hopeful, old age fruitful, and death acceptable, honorable, even great.

Today I'll look into my body and soul to find what I am most passionate about. I'll begin to remember that I am an enthusiastic and passionate man.

99. Our Stories Are Mirrors

APRIL 8

No story is the same to us after the lapse of time: or rather we who read it are no longer the same interpreters.
— George Eliot (Mary Ann Evans)

The stories I share with other men—how I was wounded, went crazy, hit bottom, started healing, what I do these days to get sane—are a great form of service. These stories are mirrors for others, reflecting their progress, and giving them a glimpse of future health. Listening to my story, they hear their own pain—and a promise.

In our common stories, ancient answers to timeless questions are revealed. From the personal sharing in a Twelve Step meeting to the archetypes found in a tale from Grimm, the stories we tell reflect the essence of our struggles and our joys. We're just now beginning to understand our great need to tell our stories, and to feel our pain at last. Some may say they are tired of hearing stories of suffering. But where would I be today, and how would I have begun to heal, if everyone who heard my pain had been too tired to listen?

Today I'll listen closely to the stories of other men. When the opportunity arises, I'll share with others. If I'm restless or bored, I'll offer that as part of my story. My story is a mirror, and everything has a right to be reflected in it.

100. The Perfection of Imperfection

Baseball . . . teaches that errors are part of the game.

—Ernest Kurtz

Some of us, long ago, learned that anything less than perfection was failure. We learned this in our families, at school, from coaches. Some of us had "four A, one B" parents: we handed them our report card, they looked silently at the row of A's, then saw the B and said, "What is *this* doing here?" Such parents pass on to their children the intolerance they got from their own parents. As adults they teach their children to be ashamed of anything less than perfection, even if their children are doing very well.

If our worst fear is to make an error, we can't make any home runs either. When we feel our worth depends on perfection, we stop taking risks. But if we can't risk failure, our days will be colorless and empty.

Inevitably our life's journey will include stumbling over rough terrain. At these rough spots we discover our inner strength. Besides, without our "mistakes," we'd be somewhere else—we'd be some-*one* else! Today, we can try to accept all we've lived through. We can keep going, accepting the outcome, whether it matches our fantasies or not.

Today I'll look back on my "mistakes" with new eyes. All that I've done in my life has helped me to arrive where I am right now.

101. Grief

> *The only nourishment*
> *He knew was grief, endless in its hidden*
> *   source*
> *Yet never-ending hunger.*
> *   —The Epic of Gilgamesh*

Grief is a natural response to loss. This deep and common feeling among men can be individually helpful, as well as community-building. Men sharing grief can feel deeply connected. Yet men today do not have permission and support to express grief. When a family loses a loved one, the men are expected to be strong for the entire family, rather than feel or express their own feelings. We are often asked to hold up the family and hold on to our own feelings, rather than discharge them.

After centuries of holding grief in, many men are out of touch not only with this feeling but with other feelings as well. The poet Robert Bly asserts, "Grief is the doorway to men's feelings." Many people think that doorway is anger, since men more often express anger; but anger is often a cover-up for sorrow, longing, sadness, grief.

Expressing grief can free a man. Opening to grief can help us open to a range of feelings. As the grief returns and is expressed it brings a variety of feelings that had gone underground. The ability to grieve can help preserve the ability to love.

Today I will explore my grief, admit it, and allow it to be expressed. I know I will come to its end and be in a changed state.

102. On Being Happy

Dwell as near as possible to the channel in which your life flows.

—Henry David Thoreau

Many men believe that happiness can be made the same way a microchip, or a bale of hay, or a beautiful painting is made. We've been taught and shown that happiness is a small thing, a by-product of what we accomplish and achieve. If we're not happy, we tend to think it's because of something we've left undone or done poorly. If we can only discover what we did wrong and correct it, we'll become happy.

Perhaps we don't understand the nature of happiness at all. Perhaps it's not something we're in charge of. Maybe we can't create it or control it.

The word *happiness* comes from the root of the word "happens." In other words, "happiness" comes from what "happens," not from what we do or make. If a child "happens" our way, smiles at us, and lets us give him a big hug, then that's what is happening. Such a moment is a form of happiness. And so is the sunrise we watch on a crisp morning, the lunch date filled with the laughter of friends, a tender late-night conversation with a lover, and yes, the promotion that finally comes.

Today, watching what happens with a clearer eye, I'll let the moments of this day produce their happiness in me. Practicing this natural happiness, I can stop trying to buy, build, earn, or make it.

103. Priorities

Men understand the worth of blessings only when they have lost them.

—Plautus

It is important for us to take stock of what is valuable in our life. The swiftness of time often blurs our ability to stay attuned to what is really important.

There is an exercise that helps us stop to see our ongoing life from a fresh perspective. The technique is to list the people we would contact and the things we would do if we learned that we had only one week left to live. Seldom do such items as "Work harder" or "Spend time with people I don't like" appear on the list. Instead the list more likely includes spending time with loved ones, or making an effort to tell these people that we love them and appreciate them. Whenever we do this exercise, we realize that the people in our life, and the love and gratitude we have for them, have always been most important of all.

Today I will write down the things I would do if I had only one week to live.

104. Poetry

Poetry lies beyond seriousness, on that more primitive and original level where the child, the animal, the savage and the seer belong, in the region of dream, enchantment, ecstasy, laughter.

—Johan Huizinga

Some say that poetry was born at sea, when the wind took the words. Or in the mouths of babes, given to rhyming. "Give me back the soul I had as a child," the great Spanish poet Federico García Lorca implores. Poetry comes from the soul of children. Poetry is sacred play and magic. Whatever its origin, poetry is a gift of the human soul, tied closely to song. The root word for poetry comes from a word that means "to make." Poetry is making.

Poetry has no function; it just is. Poetry is ritual, rhythm, word, breath and pause, entertainment, artistry, trickery, riddle-making, persuasion, sorcery, fiction, and prophecy. Poets are possessed, smitten; they rave and love. Poetry precedes prose and is closer to the heart.

Today I will play with words, perhaps in the form of verse, or perhaps in some other form. I may choose to make a present of my words, either to myself or to another person.

105. Praise

To praise is the whole thing.
                    —Rainer Maria Rilke

When was the last time I was truly and thoroughly praised? We each deserve praise. When was the last time I praised someone else? Others deserve it, too. Praising, either way, helps us to continue and to expand. It adds vigor. Many of us hear more criticism than praise. Exercising the voice that praises helps enliven the entire spirit. Life itself is a miracle, and each day is miraculous, worthy of our praise. How precious it is to be alive! The ancients praised with many of their psalms.

Objects of praise can include persons, places, feelings, and memories. From the tiny to the huge, all deserve our praise. Praise can awaken and ignite. It can help set fire. Appreciation is a food that helps one grow.

Today I will praise someone, something, someplace. I may elect to praise myself. I also open myself to hear any praise that may come my way.

106. Financial Fears

*In the dark times, will there also be singing?
Yes, there will also be singing about the dark
times.*

—Bertolt Brecht

When money is scarce, sometimes I search my mind about where I'd get financial help if I really needed it. Thinking this way, I begin to feel lonely, as though it's all up to me. I may have parents who could make a loan if necessary, but such loans often come with strings attached, and unspoken expectations. My ideas for financial relief begin to seem pale and beside the point. Like it or not, being broke puts me in touch with the real Source of all I have.

If my sinking dinghy is to stay afloat until my "ship comes in," I must relinquish my claim to be captain, and alert the crew that we all must keep bailing, praying, and simply staying with the boat.

More often than not, I have plenty of company on that boat. It's the fear that can overcome me like a tidal wave. This fear must be felt and released from my mind and body, just like any other feeling. If I do this, other men will join me in support. As I openly share my fear of "sinking," the terror I've carried so long in the pit of my stomach will subside. Then I'm empty and simple again. I remember, "In God We Trust."

Today I will own my financial fears, and share them with another man. Remembering together, we can look to the real Captain of our ship for lasting help.

107. The Sacred Inner Space

There is a place within us that can never be tarnished.

—Pir Vilayat Inayat Khan

No matter what has happened to me in the past, no matter what I've done, inside of me is a sacred space. It's a part of me that can't be limited by my mind or my body. This place exists inside me at all times, wherever I am. Beyond the self-doubt, the pain and insecurity, beyond even the joy of life, this sacred space inside connects me to the expansive perfection of the universe.

When men come together to pray, meditate, chant, drum, or share with open hearts in any endeavor, we meet each other on a deep level. In that place we meet without competition or conflict, taking our satisfaction from this shared inner reservoir of grace.

Today I honor the sacredness that exists in myself and all others.

108. I Am Many Men

*The pleasures of heaven are with me, and the
     pains of hell are with me,
The first I graft and increase upon myself. . . .
     the latter I translate into a new tongue.*
                              —Walt Whitman

Some mornings my soul is so quiet, I can hear a leaf drop through the branches of the oak tree just outside my bedroom window. I can sense the cool water in the stream that stretches all the way through the valley. I can listen to the infinite play of wind chimes.

Then there are days when a barking dog makes me want to bark back, louder. When serenity is tenuous, even the sound of a plane passing at thirty-five thousand feet can be enough to ruin the morning.

On both kinds of days, the noisy and the quiet, the same challenge exists: to accept and, yes, even love whatever is taking place inside me. To see myself as many men, to practice loving these seemingly opposite parts of myself is to begin to learn real love.

Today I offer love to the many different men in me, both the ones I've met and the ones I still don't know.

109. Respect for Ourselves

Some trees grow very tall and straight and large in the forest close to each other, but some must stand by themselves or they won't grow at all.

—Oliver Wendell Holmes

"Men have trouble expressing emotions." "Men are aggressive, aren't they—always compelled to work and produce." "Men are builders, not dreamers." The list of stereotypes we've learned and embodied goes on and on. Limiting our expectations of ourselves to these caricatures is a form of repression. When we break out of the box, people are often surprised, even angry, that we changed the script. Living a stereotype means giving up our true selves, and subordinating our intuition to a rigid set of rules. When that happens, we severely limit our ability to be authentic.

Each one of us expresses himself uniquely. One day a man may not be able to express his feelings, but later he may be deeply expressive. Some days he may be a warrior, some days a peacemaker. We demean ourselves by conforming to stereotypes. We are individuals, with all the intricacy and variety that implies.

When I expand my awareness beyond the masculine stereotypes I've been taught, I'll become much more aware of who I really am and who I am becoming.

110. Rhythm

Rhythm is the soul of life. The whole universe revolves in rhythm. Everything and every human action revolves in rhythm.
—Babatunde Olatunji

In the beginning, even before the word, was rhythm. The heartbeat and blood flowed throughout our bodies. Things revolve throughout the cosmos in constant motion. Everything is in movement and we, individually and collectively, are part of that movement. At the smallest levels of atoms and molecules, as well as at the largest levels of universes, the component parts are always moving, circulating. That motion is the life force.

As a boy you probably tapped—perhaps fingers to knees. You tapped on the floor as you crawled along. It is common in boys and girls to tap, until that life rhythm is interrupted by adults. As adult men we can regain our boy's natural body movements and the sounds that they produce. All we have to do is go out and get a drum—a drum of our own. It could be an African conga that sits on the ground. Or a Native American hoop drum. Or a Middle Eastern ceramic drum. There are many kinds of drums. Find yours. It could even be your stomach. Stomachs make good drums.

Today I will join the universal rhythm of which I am already a part.

111. Ritual

The purpose of ritual is to wake up the old mind in us, to put it to work. The old ones inside us . . . have been ignored.
—Z. Budapest

Many kinds of rituals exist—to open and close gatherings, to mark changing seasons, and to honor rites of passage such as marriage and death. Rituals draw individuals into a sense of shared community. Rituals are containers; they hold, enclose, protect. Doing rituals with men can build brotherhood and friendship based on more than just the personal and personality. Respect, care, and love can grow among men in ritual, amidst differences of age, race, culture, politics, status.

Many kinds of men's groups exist— for fun, for work, for growth and development. A men's ritual group is a distinct kind of group. Ritual helps us see beyond ourselves to realize that there is something out there separate from us with which we can connect. In ritual we can enter the worlds of animals, plants, and mythology. Something happens in ritual that can't be put into words. Men can benefit from ritual, ritual groups, and a ritual life—to open to deeper parts of ourselves. Daily life is not enough. Ritual is needed to take us to other worlds, to which each man must go if he is to be complete.

Make a ritual for yourself or others today. It need not be too complicated. Experiment.

112. Fathering Myself

Discontent is the first step in the progress of a man or nation.

—Oscar Wilde

Some days I long so much for a father that my bones cry out for the hugs my father could not give. On those days I stay alert, because there's a danger that I may act like a son to the people in my life. My yearning can turn every man I see—my boss, my buddy, a co-worker—into that father. I may look to my lover, even to my children, for the paternal love I missed.

I have a choice to stop being a "son" with others, to stop waiting for a Magic Dad to appear. I can even stop expecting my father to *be* that dad, and just let him be who he is. This is not the simplest choice; it involves courage and grief, a whole constellation of dreams and emotions. But it is the *healthy* choice, and I'll stick with it.

Today I'll be my own father. If I catch myself turning into a "son" with others in my life, I'll gently stop myself and become my own patient parent.

113. Choices

Life is the way you see it.
—Marcus Aurelius

Black is black and white is white. These are absolutes; they are unchanging. Neither one is negative or positive, I am the one who chooses to attach a value or judgment to either color. The choices I make are the combined result of my past experiences and my present state of mind. One day I may choose to see black as positive; another day I may choose white. Later, I may decide that gray, too, has its benefits.

I make the choice. By changing my outlook, I make my world kind or cruel, confusing or simple, ugly or beautiful. As my mind changes, so does my experience.

I have a choice to redefine what I believe is masculine and manly. Having outgrown the old images and ideas, I can choose a new definition of manhood that makes sense in light of my expanding awareness. My masculinity can grow along with me.

Today I will examine the choices I make that define who I am as a man.

114. Separating and Merging

Love, in its different aspects, is as much a form of separation as of merging.
—Daniel Dean Shulman

Separation from another can bring joy as well as pain. When we leave, it can be quite pleasurable. Refusing to separate, staying too long, can bring great pain. Knowing when to separate and when to merge are key.

Men and women often have different needs regarding coming together and separating, or what we may call merging and emerging. These differences go back to childhood. In most families the primary caregiver of children is the mother. A girl learns to be a woman by identifying with her mother. The boy's process is the opposite; to become a man he must separate from, rather than identify with, his primary caregiver, his mother. So when an adult man and an adult woman meet, he is predisposed to find himself through his separateness from her and she through identification and merging. Both ways must be respected. We men need to honor our own feelings of separation and to find ways to act on those feelings. This means understanding our need to separate and communicating about that need with our loved ones. There are many ways of separating, some of which enable connection.

What do I need to let go of . . . to leave . . . to separate from? From what part of myself do I need to disengage? Is there someone hanging on who is draining me, from whom I need to separate?

115. Service

The greatest use of life is to spend it for something that will outlast it.
—William James

What of my life will last beyond my death? Certainly not the material possessions I've acquired, or the honors I've accumulated. All these toys and laurels are left behind and eventually fall to dust. My true contribution is invisible: what I pass on to others in the form of love, guidance, support, and acceptance.

It is truly the little kindnesses that count. When I listen to the words of someone younger, when I help a frustrated child, when I support and accept a friend through hard times, I am engaged in timeless, deathless acts. For when I touch other people with love, that kindness is passed on to their friends, their children, and their children's children. Love, by its nature, expands, like ripples in a pond.

Today I honor my life's service: I will look for an opportunity to do a simple kindness.

116. Reaching Out

APRIL 25

The real friend . . . is, as it were, another self.

—Marcus Tullius Cicero

I feel swamped on days when so many people seem to depend on me—wife, child, boss, friend, aging parents. I want to reach out for solid ground, asking, "What about me? I'm drowning in a sea of responsibility!"

Today I'll teach my arms to reach out to a brother, a safe man who will listen. I'll let myself take in his supportive embrace with my full body and being. I'll risk telling him how much I hurt, how much I need, how much I love.

Today I'll explore a long-forgotten masculine way. By reaching out to another man, I reach deeper into myself.

117. Wisdom

I look deep into my heart,
to the core where wisdom arises.
Wisdom comes from the Unnameable
and unifies heaven and earth.
            —Psalm 121 (translated by Stephen
                                        Mitchell)

Many kinds of wisdom exist, contemporary and ancient, of the mind and of the body. Each animal and each plant has wisdom to impart to men. At each age we have distinct wisdom, which is not reserved for elders alone. Infants have a wisdom of the oneness of all, which few adults retain. As a child crawls he develops another wisdom. Each step—acquiring language, for example—has its own wisdom. Some children are "wise beyond their years." Be sure to learn from such people. A multigenerational community has access to substantial wisdom, as does the man who lives naturally in communication with other cultures, especially the wild ones.

   Each culture or subculture has its own wisdom. Male and female subcultures, for example, have retained certain forms of unique knowledge. Each group of people has a special wisdom for our planet. Let us honor that wisdom.

What wisdom do I have? Who might I share it with today? What wisdoms do I seek? Where might I encounter them?

118. Milestones

We must use time creatively . . . and forever realize that the time is always ripe to do right.
—Martin Luther King, Jr.

The life which is unexamined is not worth living.

—Plato

Like a long road, my life is marked by milestones: important events or times of transition. Birthdays are milestones; so are the deaths of friends or other loved ones. I may pass through many transitions on my journey—marriage, divorce, the birth of a child, a sudden change in my state of health. Whatever milestones are, it is important that I pause to reflect on them. If all that happens to me passes by unnoticed, what will I have learned? What will I have to pass on?

By reflecting on the milestones in my life, I can better understand my true position in this world. I can see the flow of time and the process of my existence. Sensing the continuity of my life, I can take comfort that I am a part of a larger whole. Others share, in spirit, the same milestones I experience. Truly, we are all in this together.

Today I will stop to reflect on a recent milestone in my life.

119. Not Striving

It is not healthy to be thinking all the time. Thinking is intended for acquiring knowledge or applying it. It is not essential living.
—Ernest Wood

As young men we love to "push the river," trying out our mental and physical muscles, swimming against the current. Older men want a rest, so they look for a way to jump in and ride the swift waters. Early on we learned that our lives were up to us, that we should strive hard, persevere, even punish our bodies to keep our heads above water. We forgot that we could be held up by that water, made alive by its grace, supported by its buoyant energy.

Few of us learned the secret of freedom: that "not-doing" carries us further than we could ever have gone under our own efforts. Even better, when we stop pushing our lives along, the ego stays in check, because it can't take credit for what we accomplish by letting go.

Nature teaches "not-doing" to all men with eyes to see. The chick does not construct the egg it's born from. The grass is planted by the wind, the lake is filled by the rain, and no one has to wake up the sun in the morning! Life has its perfect plan. When we surrender to its current, we're free to rest our mental machinery.

Today I explore the idea of "not-doing." I can let my work unfold on its own, my children grow up in their own time. If I can let go of controlling the details, my life will open its mysteries to me.

120. Women and Men Together

We must try to trust one another. Stay and cooperate.

—Jomo Kenyatta

All men and women are brothers and sisters. We share the Earth, drink the same water, breathe the same air. All women and all men are engaged in an ongoing partnership that guides and directs the entire human species. Through misuse of power, manipulation, and misunderstanding on both sides, the bond between men and women has been weakened, leading us to the brink of environmental disaster, starvation, and warfare.

Now it is time for all of us to heal. Men and women must work together, sharing power, compassion, and love. The future of our world and the lives of our children depend on it. There is great hope in the world now. Men and women are healing their inner wounds, working together as never before. It isn't unrealistic, it isn't too late, to make this world better, for men, women, and children.

Today I will consciously bring open-mindedness, compassion, and respect to my relationships with women.

121. Wounds as Gifts

We may imagine our deep hurts not merely as wounds to be healed but as salt mines from which we gain a precious essence and without which the soul cannot live.

—James Hillman

All men are wounded. We are all casualties. Our wounds can become gifts. The wounds happened, perhaps long ago, and there is not much we can do about what actually caused them. However, a lot can be done regarding our response to the wounds and the relationship of the wounds to our present life. Some people ignore their wounds. Others dwell on them. Finding the right balance of attention is key—not allowing the wounds to dominate our lives, either by going underground or by remaining too much in the foreground.

A man ignores his wounds at great peril. Wounds denied are likely to fester. Untended wounds can infect others—in one's family, at work, or in one's circle of friends. Our tasks as men include the mending of our wounds, transforming them into gifts that can feed the soul.

Today I will contemplate the ways in which I have been wounded. What are the particular wounds that have helped define me? How might I transform these wounds into gifts?

122. The Dance of Healing

It does not matter how slowly you go, so long as you do not stop.

—Confucius

Two steps forward, one step back: This is the pattern of the healing dance. But it's a pattern we men may be uncomfortable with, because this is one dance we can never lead. The healing process itself must show us the new moves. In order to heal, I must sometimes follow, but if I find I don't know how to follow, then I must learn. Perfectionism gets in the way when I'm trying to become healthier. Progress takes time. I must practice—in my relationships, with family, friends, and partners—before I stop stepping on toes and begin to move with grace.

Today I'll accept that backward motion is a natural part of the dance of healing. As I learn to join the flow of each moment, as I practice compassion for myself, I'll discover the freedom that exists in following well.

123. Wilderness

The clearest way into the Universe is through a forest wilderness.

—John Muir

We've given up so much in order to live in cities, to ride enclosed in metal, hurtling along so fast we can't see the landscape. Our reliance on fast food, electric power, and soundproof walls has moved us beyond the reach of nature, far from the elemental forces of life that form our most basic heritage. We may not want to return to living in a cave by torchlight, but if we are to keep our perspective in this wide universe, we must seek out wild places.

We must go to the mountains, to the sea, to the untouched and unspoiled places. It's there that we find a grand design for our own lives. We experience the ebb and flow of the tides, the wind blowing free, and the deep, uncertain darkness of night. In the wild places we feel the cycles of nature and experience with clarity nature's movements, that continuous juggling of life and death. Surrounded by the wild forces, our vision stays fresh, and we remember humility, seeing our true size in this world.

Today I will seek a wild place where my soul can feel its roots, and experience its freedom.

124. Trees

It seems as if the story of my life is the story of trees I've loved. Some remain standing. Others fell down.

—Deena Metzger

The waving branches of a tall maple tree strokes the sky as if caressing an invisible body. The wind animating the branches seems to have intention. The branches reach toward us as though offering their blessing. There are many different kinds of trees, which vary by size, shape, smell, and sight. Their trunks, branches, and leaves are distinct. They offer us many opportunities.

Reaching from the ground into the sky, trees weld the universe together, providing miraculous beauty. You can climb in them, even as an adult. They offer cover. Trees change with the seasons, carrying on vital processes that help keep us alive in body and soul, even when we ignore them. There is much in this universe that supports us without our acknowledgment. It is time to honor trees and their gifts to us.

Do you have a favorite tree—a kind of tree or a particular tree? When was the last time you planted a tree? And then saw it grow? What is your relationship to trees?

Today I allow myself to be comforted by the beauty and the feel of trees.

125. Mountains

I stood by the river and looked up at the mountains. Suddenly a deep voice, vibrant with suppressed emotion, spoke from behind me into my left ear. "Do you not think all life comes from the mountain?"

—Carl G. Jung

Mountains are always there—sturdy. As life swirls about, mountains remain, changing, but oh so slowly. Near Ghost Ranch in northern New Mexico the mountains are exposed and open; the different colors reveal the years, many millions, over which these immense beings have emerged. Mountains hold great stories, which good listeners can hear, if they bend their ears to the earth. Go find a mountain, outside or inside, place your ear upon it, and listen to it. What do you hear?

While looking at such mountains in the Southwest, Aldo Leopold suggested that we "think like a mountain." When we do, we can access great wisdom—not the wisdom of *doing* but the wisdom of *being*. Mountains have much to teach us, simply by being. Their knowing is ancient and carries with it the ragged and eruptive wisdom of the ground.

Today I will look at a mountain—either in reality, in my mind, or in a picture. What do I see? What can I learn from this mountain? What is its teaching for me?

126. The Sea

Each admirable genius is but a successful diver in that sea whose floor of pearls is all our own.
—Ralph Waldo Emerson

Take a trip to the sea—in actuality or in your imagination. Imagine a large body of water, whose beginning you can see and that reaches beyond your sight. Now listen to the sounds it makes. What do those sounds remind you of? Notice the color of the water—sometimes blue, other times more green. Notice where the water meets the soil, and the sand and the coast that are created.

What is carried by the water? Do you see plants, logs, anything else? Can you imagine yourself, now looking at the water, now beneath it? From that underwater perspective how does the world appear different? What do you like the most about the ocean? Its power? Its sound? Its mystery? Perhaps you can get in a boat with oars, or with a sail, or with a motor and move across the waters. How does it feel? Or perhaps you can move swiftly across the water, skiing, noticing how it holds you, yet allows you to fall softly into it. We are always surrounded by water, which provides a gentle yet powerful context for life. Water is the fluid, constantly changing aspect of life.

Today I will swim in the sea of my mind to discover what gifts I can encounter there. I will seek forgotten memories now ready to emerge from the sea of my unconsciousness.

127. Rivers

The fountains mingle with the river,
*   And the rivers with the ocean . . .*
Nothing in the world is single;
*   All things, by a law divine,*
In one spirit meet and mingle. . . .
                    —Percy Bysshe Shelley

Rivers do many things. They carry water, animals, wood, and sometimes human pain and grief. When we are sad, a river can be a healing place to deposit sorrow. Rivers have meaning in various religious traditions. For example, at Rosh Hashanah, the Jewish New Year, Jews cast bread upon the river, symbolically releasing their wrong deeds.

Rivers contain great mystery. Where did this particular river come from? Where is it going? Rivers can lead us to reflect on where we came from and where we are going. Who else stands by this river's side? Rivers vary—some are relatively straight, others have a snaking, winding quality about them. Rivers can deepen contemplation. Rivers can define boundaries, dividing nations, states, towns. Rivers and riversides are great sources of life and vitality, as the green that surrounds them testifies. Rivers rise and fall, varying with seasons.

What rivers do you recall in your life? You may want to say their names out loud or write them down. How did they influence you? Sitting by the edge of a river, we can drink in its ancient sounds, stories, and wisdoms.

Today I may choose to develop my relationship with a body of water—a pond, bay, or river.

128. The Language of Animals

Animals are nothing but the forms of our virtues and vices, wandering before our eyes, the visible phantoms of our souls.

—Victor Hugo

Men used to listen attentively to the messages of the animals; our lives, our souls, depended on it. The appearances and absences of certain animals at certain times were full of meaning, and offered essential guidance. The hawk, raven, wolf, and bear all sent messages to men and spoke in a language we understood.

A part of us still understands that language. The animals still speak, showing up at interesting times, in "coincidental" ways. A husky, a cousin to the wolf, might walk up to us just when we are in need of courage. A cat visits when we require patience. When peace is most precious, a dove flies overhead. The animals are speaking.

Today I'll observe the animals, to absorb their wisdom.

129. Friends

Only friends will tell you the truths you need to hear to make . . . your life bearable.
                    —Francine du Plessix Gray

How many men do you really have in your life that you can talk to? Five? Three? One? Maybe you think you can really share openly with many of your men friends, but is this really the case? When do you reach out?

Take a pencil and a piece of paper and list the men whom you can really talk to. These are men who have heard your story, who have seen you at your best and at your worst. They are the men you count on to support you in hard times.

How many men appear on your list? Now note the date of the last time you really had an in-depth conversation with each of these men. Are you really experiencing friendship with these men, or are you content just to be aware that they're there? If you don't actively share with them what is important to you, on a regular basis, what is your relationship to them?

Today I will call one of my men friends, just to make contact with him.

130. True Family

The one guardian of life is love, but to be loved you must love.

—Marsilio Ficino

True family is more a matter of love than blood. Some of us have few or no blood relatives, and others have many relatives but feel as disconnected from them as we are from strangers.

Our true family may be a mixture of relatives and fellow travelers. The true family may simply end up being whoever doesn't vanish when we enter recovery. In one sense, our family is made up of people who accept us as we are, with all our quirks, our sweetness, our orneriness, and our vulnerability. True family doesn't try to change us; they listen with real interest to all the changes we're going through. They don't judge us if we're stuck in old behaviors. And they share their struggles with us, so we have our chance to offer support, to give something back.

In a true family, we love each other the way we need to love and be loved. We have no secrets but speak truthfully to each other, and work it out if hurt feelings arise. To be part of a real family, we have to unlock our fears and *live*. Only then will there be room for the fun and love that arises from just being ourselves.

Today I can choose to create my own family. If this family doesn't include all my biological kin, I need not feel guilty.

131. Caring for Men

MAY 10

I got active in the men's movement partly because I realized, now in my fifties, that we men need to take care of each other.
  —Harry Faddis, Redwood Men's Center

Barriers exist that prevent men from caring for men or being cared for by them. Caring tends to be the domain of women in our culture. The men's movement is creating environments where men can feel comfortable caring for each other. Such care can be distinct from that of women. A father's care for a child, for example, differs from a mother's. Fathers and children delight in various games—such as throwing the child playfully into the air and catching him or her. Men's care can have a positive, letting-be quality.

Men have society's permission to care for each other only in certain situations: At funerals we are permitted to care and even to cry. In battle we care for each other; survival depends upon it. Sometimes men are called upon to care for aging parents. Athletes can also care for each other. Farmers help each other in caring ways. In certain Latin and Mediterranean cultures men tend to feel greater ease at touching each other—even kissing affectionately on the cheeks—than in Anglo-dominated cultures. We could all benefit from widening permission for men to care not only for women and children, but also for other men.

Whom might I care for today? How can I express that care?

132. Welcoming Our Challenges

Weary the path that does not challenge.
                                        —Hosea Ballou

So often we welcome Happiness and Joy as visiting gods, but shun Pain and Grief as terrible demons. We welcome what is predictable and pleasant, and avoid that which could challenge and strengthen us. For challenges often come in the form of crises. Some of these crises almost killed us as kids; they still hurt even now in memory.

But if we welcome the call to grief when it comes, our masculinity will be more deeply formed. We become courageous men who accept the need to face whatever comes. If we deny the grief of this life, we mask our manhood. But if we embrace pain as an honorable guest, a teacher, and a guide, we accept the challenge of manhood that leads to wisdom.

Today I will welcome Grief as a temporary guest in my being. I'll remember that Grief always comes bearing gifts: lessons in life and healing. When this guest leaves, I'll make room for the other distinguished visitors: Faith, Hope, and Joy.

133. Rest

How beautiful it is to do nothing, and then rest afterward.

—Spanish proverb

"Work!" "Produce!" "Get busy!" "Earn your way!" "Hold your own!" "Carry your own weight!" These and other messages about business and work have been drilled into our male consciousness since we were boys. Doing nothing and resting was "unmanly," a "waste of time." Even as adults, it's almost inconceivable for most of us to "do nothing, and then rest." What rest we do take often is merely preparation to work harder and earn more. We go on vacation because it will increase productivity; we take a rest break because it will enable us to work longer hours. Where is the rejuvenation in this kind of "rest"?

Doing nothing has its own virtues and rewards. When we're quiet and still for a while, our awareness of ourselves and the world around us changes. Time seems to slow down, and we have room to enjoy ourselves and our lives. Things seem less serious, less all-important. We can take delight in "being a man" rather than just "doing and producing" full-time. We have a natural inner clock that tells us when it's time for work, but we can't hear it unless we are still enough to become aware of its presence.

Today I'll take some time to do nothing. Then I'll rest.

MAY 13

Every man is an omnibus in which his ancestors ride.

—Oliver Wendell Holmes

Lack of connection with one's personal legacy is a key cause of isolation. Reestablishing contact with our male ancestors, even when doing so requires pushing through resistance and darkness, can help break that isolation and aid in the recovery of the Deep Masculine. Affirming our roots, and accepting any tangles we find there, can help bring us back into community.

We can do much to recover our male legacy. We can look at pictures of our ancestors and imagine what their lives may have been like. We can read about the times in which they lived. We can listen to stories from other family members, or we tell stories of our own, real or imagined. Getting in touch with our male lineage— the men who came before us and who now reach across the years to touch our lives—can be profoundly healing.

We will all be ancestors someday. Coming to know our predecessors helps us recognize our connection—and our responsibility—to the generations that will follow.

How do I want to be remembered? What can I do today to be the kind of ancestor I would like to be?

135. Uncle

I spent many summers in my childhood on a farm with an uncle who told stories endlessly. This was his method of working the raw material of his life.

—Thomas Moore

"One who helps, advises or encourages" is one way the dictionary defines uncle. The root word for avuncular means "maternal uncle." In many traditional societies it is the mother's brother who initiates boys into manhood. Uncles have a closeness to the boy; a special love and intimacy can arise from that closeness. Uncles have some distance, because they do not have to discipline the boy. Uncles can be playful and entertaining, as well as educational. We can all benefit from an uncle and his active participation in our lives.

Uncles can be great! With an inner Uncle as our guide, the Deep Masculine is strengthened. Each boy (and girl) needs an image in his (her) inner life of such a Deep Masculinity. Find that image for yourself.

Go inside. Who is your helpful, encouraging Uncle? Stretch if you cannot find someone within your family. Bring him to awareness now. If you did not have him in the outer world, construct him now in the inner world.

136. The Rhythm of Mother

How we enter into love and behave in closeness and nearness . . . all bear the marks of mother.

—James Hillman

The way we were mothered as boys says a lot about how we love today as men. Our relationship with Mother affects the degree to which we're able to let others love us, and for how long.

Of course, we began learning the rhythms of Mother long before we ever saw her face. Inside her womb, we received into our bodies her food and drink, and her feelings. Even at this early stage, we were already taking into ourselves our mother's hopes and fears about us. Our body still remembers those delicate undercurrents in the waters of the womb. Part of our struggle as men is to divide our feelings and our desires from those of Mother. No wonder it is so difficult sometimes!

Today we're establishing our own rhythm of closeness to others, one that's independent of Mother's rhythms. All we have to guide us in this task is the deep knowing inside ourselves. If we go gently within, we can rest in the Womb of our inner Self. By learning the rhythms of the Great Mother within us, we bring greater truth and health into our intimacy with others.

Today, as I move out of childhood patterns, I begin to really listen to myself, and to follow the movements within my own being. I will honor the love I received from my mother, but will find ways to leave the unhealthy rhythms behind.

137. Fun

I decided to make a circus just for the fun of it.
—Alexander Calder

This world can seem complex and demanding. Between work, parenting, community activities, and my inner search for where I fit into it all, there seems little time to relax. My activities reward me with a sense of accomplishment and fulfillment, but I don't always feel I'm having *fun*. My life is already meaningful, but where is the fun, the pleasure, the excitement?

Just hanging out, talking with others, can bring pleasure and happiness. Being with other men, joking and laughing about life and its mysteries, can be fun. I want to play and to create for the sheer joy of it. My life is full of opportunities for fun. My work, my daily interactions with others, can be full of loving playfulness. The fun, the play, lies in how I choose to see things.

Today I will have fun right where I am, whatever I am doing.

138. Waking in the Dark

One does not discover new lands without losing sight of the shore for a very long time.
—André Gide

My search for wholeness requires that I "wake up." Sometimes the waking is slow, and sometimes it is sudden, but when I wake I'm often startled at what I find. I've come to a critical crossroads and I'm completely baffled: the old ways of being no longer work, and the new ways are still untried—perhaps even uninvented.

So often we're afraid to hesitate, to pause and reflect before choosing our direction. Our old definition of masculinity tells us, "Move on! Get going; you're shirking your responsibilities!" We misinterpret any uncertainty as weakness. Yet these are the very times that offer us the opportunity to gain a new understanding of who we are as men. In such moments, our souls are strengthened.

Today I won't be caught in an archaic web of "shoulds." I'll explore my feelings of uncertainty, get to know them. I will yield to that instinctive part of myself that always knows the way.

139. Emptying

Just as there is fire in wood, there is peace within this body.
                    —Gurumayi Chidvilasananda

We have been taught our whole lives that we should never be found wanting. We have thought of emptiness as a state to avoid at all costs. We've been told to *fill*, and to be *fulfilled*, never really understanding what these words meant. We've been counseled and conditioned to consume all we can. In our quest for excellence and excitement, we even begin to treat people as commodities rather than companions.

And yet when we release the anger from our body, when we dip into our well of grief to bring out that bitter water, we always feel the amazing freedom of emptiness. Full of greed, grief, alcohol, and ice cream, it is very difficult to feel delighted and free. Emptying my body and soul of all that is unnecessary releases the great possibilities, the great potential within us.

Today I will go a new way—toward emptiness —with trust that, in that still place, I will find everything I truly need.

140. Surrender

The ancient saying,
  "Surrender brings perfection,"
  is not just an empty phrase.
Truly, to the surrendered comes the perfect;
  To the perfect comes the whole Universe.
  —Tao Te Ching

In basic training the Army teaches that surrender is defeat. Shame is associated with surrender. Surrender actually can be victory and a new beginning. We have to unlearn some of the things we have been taught. Surrender calls us to get out of the way so that something can happen—birth, a relationship, an artistic creation. If we surrender to our bodies, pleasure can result. If we surrender to another person, connection can occur. If we surrender to creative impulse, beauty can emerge. Surrendering to the wrong person, idea, or movement can be disastrous. Appropriate surrender can enhance life.

A man unable to surrender is unable to give. In surrendering we release. What we surrender is control, or the illusion of control. To go to sleep we have to surrender rational control over consciousness. A major cause of insomnia is the fear of surrender—of not being in control. When we let go we can open up and be more free.

To what do I need to surrender? Is there a truth that I need to accept? Who might I surrender to and, by surrendering, grow?

141. Going Off Alone

Thoreau became acquainted with the night, with the sorrow of the woods and the melancholy of the snow; he found depths and learned to trust them; he lived alone and liked the company.

—Robert Bly

A man needs to go off alone. He must. There is no other way to learn and to do certain things that a man must learn and do. All the books, partners, and helpers cannot take a man to the places where solitary exploration can lead him. All the love in the world cannot substitute for a man going off by himself. In such a solitary place he can learn more about masculine mystery. Thoreau knew this in the nineteenth century, as did Francis of Assisi in the thirteenth century, as does Robert Bly in our own time.

Other men can act as guides. Elders in particular, and children, can help a man tremendously, especially if they do not seek to entangle him. Ultimately, though, each man's journey is his own. The best help is that which sets a man free, rather than that which binds him. Being alone, especially in the night, can also change our habitual perspectives on things and can allow new insights to emerge.

Today I will imagine myself alone away from people. As I do, what knowledge moves toward me? What do I learn? Is there something now that I must do?

142. Asking

Brothers, find internal wealth. It is truly
  priceless.
Thieves can't get at it, the Government can't
  tax it—
only you will enjoy it.

         —Baba Muktananda

What do I really want—cars? An estate? A new job? A new wife or lover? A swimming pool? Kids? A million dollars? These are some of the things I was taught to trade body and soul for. While there's nothing wrong with any of them, all are secondary to the search for who I am. It's this search that fuels my life and that will determine what I *really* want.

Without knowing our innermost Self, without learning to be inwardly at rest, the mundane details of our lives can quietly overwhelm us. We wander our own land feeling totally lost. We dream and dream and never take action to manifest those dreams. We have kids hoping they'll express our lost lives for us. Without deep inner knowledge, our decisions lack the strength of conviction, and we live in reaction to our fears.

I do know what I want: simply to be myself. This is wealth beyond measure, far more satisfying than anything outside myself. I want to give myself the time to separate "what's not me" from "what is me."

Today I will seek out the people who support my transformation, who can respond with compassion when I'm vulnerable enough to ask for what I really want.

143. Values

Try not to become a man of success but rather try to become a man of value.
—Albert Einstein

Success is often measured by wealth, power, fame, and countless other forms of external evidence. But these are only the most superficial parts of our lives—what is visible and concrete. Some people believe they can know us by what they see of our external lives. And sometimes we ourselves are blinded by our external trappings, judging our personal value by what we possess.

My true value as a man is understood only on the inside, when I ask myself, What's meaningful to me. What do I think of myself? What am I most deeply committed to? What statement does my life make? In the honest quiet of solitude, I must continually ask these questions of myself, if I really want to discover my own value. What I have to offer is much more than that which can be seen from the outside.

Today I will ask myself, "What is most important to me about the life I am living?"

144. The Magical Child

We find delight in the beauty and happiness of children that makes the heart too big for the body.

—Ralph Waldo Emerson

There is a magical child in me that yearns to dance and sing! He wants to jump in the mud and roll on the ground, covering himself with the earth. He yearns to explode outward in joy and zest for life. But this child is often locked away, and he longs to be released.

I hide this wonderful child behind my work, my gloom, and my pain. As closely as I guard him, though, sometimes he still manages to escape my control, and I'm seized by the spontaneous joy of being. I'll let out a belly laugh, or do something wildly silly. This childlike part of myself can love without expectation, can discover that the world is a fascinating game. To release this child is to free my truest Self, and to live with an open heart.

Today I will consciously encourage my magical child to play and be merry in his own way. If he takes a roll in the mud, I will love him all the more.

145. A Father's Presence

A teacher affects eternity; he can never tell where his influence stops.

—Henry Adams

For many of us, our fathers weren't all they might have been; few fathers are. Many of our fathers were mostly absent from our lives. When they were around they were preoccupied with their own interests. We missed time spent in their presence. We missed learning about and experiencing male closeness and solidity. Their absence left holes in our being, in our maleness.

In our friendships with other men, we began to realize what we had been missing as children. That feeling of emptiness begins to diminish. Keeping company with other men who pay attention to us, who teach us through their presence the ways of manhood, fills the hole left by our father's absence.

Today I promise to pass on what I have learned from other men.

MAY 25

Nothing is terrible, except fear itself.
—Francis Bacon

In the course of our lives, we often find ourselves in many situations we prefer to avoid: conflict with a friend, clashing with another culture, feeling needy. It would seem easier just to slip away somehow, but this is rarely the best choice. We must stand and face the fire. Better to move through the uncomfortable feelings than move through the world of relationships with fear as our compass.

Still, we can learn that we don't have to face the flames all alone. We don't have to be fearless, either. We're free to feel anything, and to ask for all the help we need. Our masculinity is not determined by how much we accomplish alone, but rather by wisdom: when to stand alone, when to ask for help, when to shield ourselves, and when to surrender.

Today I'll practice the fine art of staying put, feeling and fully experiencing whatever comes, and asking for help when I don't know what to do.

147. Releasing Worry

Ninety percent of the things I worry about don't happen, and the other ten percent I can't do anything about anyway.

> —Heard at a Twelve Step recovery meeting

It is easy for my mind to bounce from the wreckage of the past into the wreckage of the future. My thoughts seem to gravitate toward disaster, either real or imaginary. The worries grow deeper and deeper. Eventually, I'm afraid even to tell anyone that I am worried! And all because my mind is simply going around in circles, running the same films in endless repetition while I look on, horrified.

One of the easiest ways to break this cycle of worry is to talk about my feelings to another man. Sharing them puts my worries into perspective. Often the most difficult part is just moving through my fear of expressing my feelings. But I keep practicing this, because my efforts are rewarded with deeper friendships and a greater feeling of connection to everybody.

Today I will talk to another man about what I am feeling. I won't let my worries steal my peace of mind.

148. Understanding Abandonment

Adults can't be abandoned.

—John Lee

As children many of us were abandoned by those who were supposed to have loved us the most. Even today, when someone we love goes away, that feeling of abandonment arises full force. How do we cope with that feeling? Old methods come to mind: we could throw ourselves into work, find a new lover, seek out some drug to numb the pain. We could "sell out" by doing or saying whatever might keep that loved one from leaving. But this is the worst kind of abandonment—pretending to be someone we're not, substituting a "more acceptable" version of ourselves in order to avoid pain. In doing this, we abandon ourselves and only reinflict the wounds we suffered as children.

By feeling the grief we experienced in the past, we're free to be truer to ourselves in the present. With recovery, we stop seeing our parents reflected in our loved ones, and we begin to live our relationships in the here and now. Remaining true to our own nature assures that those who stick around are those who can accept us as we are.

Today I'll tell the scared little boy in me that I'll stay with him no matter what. I won't ask him to give up parts of himself to be with me. I choose today to stay with myself, for better or for worse.

149. Claiming My Life

*I would have each one be very careful to find
out and pursue his own way, and not his
father's or his mother's or his neighbor's.*
                              —Henry David Thoreau

Isn't this *my* life? Am I not ready to live it
—to love, to speak and act as my own self,
today and every day that I am here? Many
of us wake up at age thirty, forty, or fifty
to discover we've been living someone
else's dreams. On close examination, we
may discover we have thought, acted, and
chosen our livelihoods based on what our
parents wanted. In the meantime these
dreams have become our midlife night-
mares.

In order for me to be true to myself,
and to live my own life, I must let go of
others' expectations of me. I must stay
true to my choices, and let other people
say what they will. My life can never be
dictated to me by another, either subtly or
overtly. I have the courage to let go of the
guilt and fear of disappointing others by
my decisions. My strong adherence to my
personal truth may make others uncomfortable, but I will hold fast to it, because
that inner truth is all I really have.

*Today I'll take a close look at my life to sift out
what is mine, to leave behind the remnants of
others' expectations, others' dreams. If there
are parts of my life I have stored away and
labeled "Unacceptable," I will approach them
with new eyes. I will begin taking positive,
proactive, and creative steps to reclaim them.*

150. Mistakes

The man who makes no mistakes does not usually make anything.

—Bishop W. C. Magee

Making mistakes is a natural part of living. I learn by experimentation. Every time I take a risk, or begin a new experience, there is a chance that something will go wrong. I often learn what I *do* want by finding out what I *don't*.

Somewhere in the past I learned that making a mistake was shameful and "unmanly," that to be a "real man" I had to be perfect. What a painful way to live! Perfectionism only robs us of our energy and the spontaneous enthusiasm we were born with. Now I reclaim that enthusiasm, and the natural risks that go with it.

Today I can begin again to meet the events of my life with bold creativity. I can accept my "mistakes" as gifts that show me the true direction of my life.

151. Go!

Something hidden. Go and find it.
Go and look behind the Ranges—
Something lost behind the Ranges.
Lost and waiting for you. Go!
                              —Rudyard Kipling

What calls us today? Something waits for us. There may be obstacles in our way. We will have to surmount them. The sacred is often hidden, mysterious. It lies behind something, beyond something. The holy is other. As Kipling says, we must "go and find it." The journey may be an inner one. Finding the path, and not getting distracted along the way, is key. Focus and concentration are essential. Guides can help, but they can never substitute for the internal impulse that moves us out.

Many things can block men from forward motion. Sometimes it is a voice from the past that we have internalized, a voice that says, "Don't you dare!" Sometimes we ingest substances that impede our natural processes of moving toward the sacred, or we engage in behaviors that get in our way. Fortunately, all these obstacles can be removed, because the male spirit to move ahead—to go!—is strong. We are in constant movement. Our cells are each part of a living organism and are in constant motion. Being male includes an energy that impels us toward things, to connect with them. That energy is built into our bodies. Our bodies are made to go forward, as well as to pause and rest.

Where do I want to go today? How might I get there? What do I want to do? Where am I headed?

152. War

Violence seldom accomplishes permanent and desired results. Herein lies the futility of war.
—Asa Philip Randolph

It is easier to fight for one's principles than to live up to them.

—Alfred Adler

Throughout the ages men have marched off to fight for Glory, for God, for Truth. We now stand at a time in human history when we must re-examine our reasons for waging war, as well as our duty to our fellow human beings. Does it really settle our differences to employ the gun and the bomb? What is the degree of our responsibility to protect the weak, to free the oppressed?

Every man must ask himself difficult questions about war. Because we are prepared for it with games as children, a part of us loves it. Because our friends, our sons and grandsons die in battle, we hate and fear it. Who has lived through a time of war without bearing physical and emotional scars? Each of us must seek out our personal convictions about the nature of war. Whatever we decide, we must be willing to consider the consequences of our stance.

Today I will think about war and its consequences for human beings.

153. Making Peace

Blessed are the peacemakers.

—Matthew 5:9

Many men are uncomfortable with peace, though we may like the idea. We've been programmed since childhood to prepare for war, prepare to kill or be killed. We played army at five years old, imagining sticks into submachine guns, dirt clods into grenades, pretending to sneak up on the enemy to destroy them. Later on, some of us went on to wage wars on battlefields known as gridirons. If we didn't engage in combat there, then we did with fellow classmates, particularly the ones who tried to wrestle away our girlfriends. We carried our propensity for battle into bedrooms and corporate boardrooms, believing our manhood would be won or lost there.

Without a war to fight, we rested only to prepare for the next great conflict, the next chance to "prove our strength." We came to associate peace with boredom.

I want to teach my children that peace is greater than pistols, quiet and contentment more necessary than counterattack.

Today I'll make peace with an old friend or relative I've hurt, a child I wounded with words. If nothing else, I'll declare a cease-fire with myself: I'll refuse to shame myself for learning what I was taught.

154. Hands

Things men have made with wakened hands, and put soft life into are awake through years with transferred touch, and go on glowing for long years.

—D. H. Lawrence

Notice how wonderful your hands are—how beautiful and functional. Men's hands were made to interact with the outer world, to touch, and to make things. Men's hands have a vital history of digging in the soil, working with tools, and transforming wood.

When we walk around with our hands in our pockets, we lose contact with part of ourselves. In the city, we have a greater tendency to put our hands in our pockets than we do in the wilderness. At a recent men's gathering in Atlanta a man arrived with a black eye. He explained, "I had my hands in my pockets, and I fell. The road gave it to me." Some men close themselves down by putting their hands in their pockets, often jingling coins and keys, connecting themselves to those worlds. Others have hands that move freely about in the air and toward others. Our hands can connect us. They can also protect us from threats, such as the road that would give us a black eye if we collided with it. Hands hold many memories and stories. They have much to communicate.

Today I will look at my hands. I will notice them. Hands, like all other parts of the body, merit my care and attention. They were exquisitely constructed and perform magnificently. They are full of sensation and awareness, my feelers to the outer world.

155. The Human Face

Because the human face is the primary means of our recognizing and thus identifying one another, it deserves special attention.
    —A. David Napier

Do you give your face "special attention"? Or do you take it for granted? Are you aware of its changes? After a certain age, we are responsible for our own face, how we have sculpted the clay provided at our birth with our experiences, which tend to show in wrinkles and scars.

Have you noticed the inevitable differences in the two distinct sides of your face? To see those differences, and thus learn more about yourself, cover up one side of your face with your hand, and look at the exposed side in the mirror. Then change sides. Notice the difference? You may want to ask someone else to comment on any differences he sees. You may also want to ask a friend to allow you to see the differences in his two sides.

Some faces—such as that of a despised and tyrannical leader—bring pain. Others bring us great joy, such as that of a child or a beloved one. It can be healing merely to imagine the face of a beloved one. Faces have a strong impact upon us.

Today I will give my face some "special attention." I might look at it in the mirror. Touch it. Make "faces."

156. Seeing with the Heart

JUNE 4

"Goodbye," said the fox. "And now here is my secret, a very simple secret: It is only with the heart that one can see rightly; what is essential is invisible to the eye."
—Antoine de Saint-Exupéry

At the core of every man is a heart and a heartbeat. Men's gatherings celebrate this with drumming. The drumbeats echo the heartbeat. Every man has a pulse, which can be felt at various places on his body. Drumming strengthens a man's pulse, his vital force, and puts him in touch with all of the universe.

The heart does many things—pumps blood, retains feelings, breaks, feels pain, and even sees. The heart is directly connected to the eyes, as well as to the hands, to the feet, and to all other body parts. We are a whole, one, and the heart is at the core of it all. The heart is connected to the hands, the genitals, the mind; we can act, think, and feel from our heart center.

Today I will look with my heart. What do I see? What guidance does my sight give me for what I might do today?

157. Otherness

The most precious gift that marriage gave me was this constant impact of something very close and intimate yet all the time unmistakably other, resistant—in a word, real.
—C. S. Lewis

Preserving the otherness of our love mate or work partner or child, rather than requiring that the person become more like ourselves, is essential to a healthy relationship. Diversity is a sign of a healthy ecological system—be it a twosome or a manysome. If we lose otherness, the entire system erodes, rather than evolves, and is threatened.

"Unmistakably other" is how C. S. Lewis describes it. Not another version of the self. Or a screen onto which we project parts of ourselves. Or an object. But someone outside, different, at times distant, always distinct, another subject: other. As we grow in self-confidence we can appreciate others for who they are and not need to change them for our benefit.

Today I celebrate otherness. Animals and plants are other than humans. Women are other than men. Night is other than day. I will allow the otherness of such realities to influence who I am today and what I do.

158. Honoring Fathers

When we fail to honor the father, we are severely wounded.

—Valerie Andrews

The relationships between fathers and their children are among the most damaged of our time. Americans in particular seem to reject the father and indeed any outside authority. Today we have too little of what poet Robert Bly calls the "moist father" and what Dante calls the "sweet father."

The journey back to the father can be torturous, carrying us through the barbs of shame, blame, anger, fear. It is easy to blame the father, and important to get beyond such blame. A father's blessings are crucial to growth. Without these gifts, we are damaged. A man who has not been adequately fathered may have difficulty fathering in a social sense, but also perhaps biologically as well.

If we did not get what we wanted from our biological fathers, it is possible to seek it from a father figure. We can also work on developing our inner father. By honoring fathering we can develop our own capacity to father. We must not stay stuck in dishonoring the father, even if our own fathers were inadequate. To remain at that level is to open ourselves to self-hatred. If we can embrace an outer father figure, we can generate our inner capacity to father.

Is there someone in my life now who might serve as a positive father figure for me? Or is there a way I could open myself to him and then seek him?

159. Alcoholics Anonymous

JUNE 7

AA was not invented! Its basics were brought to us through the experience and wisdom of many great friends. We simply borrowed and adapted their ideas.
— Bill W., Cofounder of Alcoholics Anonymous

Over fifty years ago, Alcoholics Anonymous was founded by two men in Akron, Ohio. These men, alcoholics themselves, shaped a vision of recovery for alcoholics that has since changed the face of spirituality in our society. From its humble beginnings, Alcoholics Anonymous (AA) has grown into a vast fellowship, with millions of members meeting together every day, all over the world.

The basis for recovery in AA is the Twelve Steps. The timeless and practical spiritual principles underlying each Step can be applied by anyone who desires to live a satisfying spiritual life.

The men who founded AA came together because they needed to recover from alcoholism. When men work together in the spirit of cooperation, guided by the highest principles, their work prospers beyond what they can dream.

Today I will honor the greatness of the men who have gone before me, who have guided me by their example and their vision.

160. Spiritual Progress

We claim spiritual progress rather than spiritual perfection.
   —*The Big Book of Alcoholics Anonymous*

The principles discussed in the next twelve readings are guideposts along the spiritual pathway. They mark our way, setting forth ideals we can strive to embody. Spiritual principles are not rigid and unyielding rules, but rather reminders of the inner work that always lies ahead. If we keep on doing the work of spiritual searching, we can expect progress. Perfection, however, lies beyond the grasp of us ordinary human beings.

Integrating these principles into daily life is not an easy task, but for many men it has certainly proved worthwhile. The many Twelve Step programs of recovery that incorporate these spiritual principles invite exploration. Approaching them with open minds, we may discover likeminded men who will support and nurture our spiritual growth. Twelve Step programs, however, may not be for everyone. Each of us will find his spiritual path somewhere. Still, the spiritual principles embodied in the Twelve Steps are universal; we will find them along any spiritual road that we take.

Today I will examine my spiritual progress.

161. The Spiritual Principle of Honesty

JUNE 9

An honest man's the noblest work of God.
—Alexander Pope

The principle of honesty can be applied to any problem in our lives that is overwhelming us. Many of us have some addictive or compulsive behavior that causes us grief and pain, that regularly steals our peace of mind. It may be workaholism, sex addiction, a need to control others, or perhaps just a general feeling that things aren't working out. Whatever our situation, change begins with the honest admission of our powerlessness over that situation.

Men often have a difficult time with the concept of powerlessness. We have been taught that success only comes from being powerful and in control. Life, however, doesn't work that way, and most of what goes on in our lives is beyond our control. We can't control the actions or moods of others; we can't control the economy. Sometimes even our own behavior and feelings seem out of our control. The honest admission of powerlessness takes the pressure off of us and opens the possibility of living life on life's terms.

Today I will make an honest appraisal of my behavior, my relationships, and my life as it is right now.

162. The Spiritual Principle of Hope

JUNE 10

In the time of trouble avert not thy face from hope, for the soft marrow abideth in the hard bone.

—Hafiz (Mohammed Shams od-Din)

A life gone out of control is a life out of balance, a life of insanity. It is insane to continue, day after day, to do things that will ultimately harm ourselves. Yet how many of us do things we really don't want to do, that we don't feel good about, such as drinking alcohol, working compulsively, smoking, or having sex, because we're afraid we'll seem unmanly if we don't. When we are consistently involved in activities we know are not good for us, our lives are out of control.

True hope rests in the belief that there is a vast and benevolent power at work in the universe that will assist us in changing self-destructive thoughts and actions. Anyone who has ever tried to change something about himself, and failed, knows that great help is needed. There is nothing more demoralizing than knowing our behavior is hurting us and our loved ones, but not being able to stop by our own resources. Hope comes from knowing we can tap into a source of limitless, unconditional love that will guide us to let go of self-destructive habits.

Today—the birthday of AA—I will open my heart and mind to the concept that there is a power greater than myself in the universe.

163. The Spiritual Principle of Faith

A man consists of the faith that is in him. Whatever his faith is, he is.

—*Bhagavad-Gita*

Faith is the foundation of a life free from compulsions. By their nature, compulsive behaviors are beyond the control of self-will. Most of us are both comforted and alienated by the thought that a power greater than ourselves, a power often called God, can bring us freedom. We are comforted, because we have exhausted our own resources and realize we truly cannot change without spiritual help. But we feel alienated from God, too, afraid or unwilling to relinquish control of our lives, no matter how much pain we are in or how much pain our behavior is causing others.

Faith asks us to step into the unknown, to rely on a force we cannot really understand or describe. This flies in the face of how most of us were taught to live. We learned that manhood meant wielding power, controlling our own destiny. The third of the Twelve Steps asks us to let go of that idea, to have faith in a Higher Power, as we understand it. It is no wonder that most of us have difficulty with this concept. But faith will work where self-will consistently fails; a very little bit of faith will go a long way.

Today I will ask for guidance and faith from my Higher Power.

164. The Spiritual Principle of Courage

This is the courage in a man: to bear unflinchingly what heaven sends.

—Euripides

We men have learned to associate courage with excelling on the field of battle: being heroic, fighting against the odds, overcoming an enemy by strength and cunning. Manly courage in our culture—in our myths, movies, and music—has largely dealt with outwardly heroic acts. Although this kind of courage is real and not to be discounted, there are other forms of courage essential to the spiritual life.

Looking inward to discover our faults and fears requires a different kind of courage. It is a brave man who can take a hard look at his life and see where he has harmed himself and others. It is not easy to place our own behaviors and our choices under the microscope. But often, once we search through the past, we're simply reminded that we're human. We have made mistakes, and some of our choices may have been harmful. None of us enjoys admitting past mistakes and examining the motives behind them, but we have to do it if we're going to stop repeating the past. To heal the pain we've caused ourselves and others, we have to look at our lives squarely, unflinchingly.

Today I will use my courage to review my past.

JUNE 13

This above all: To thine own self be true;
And it must follow, as the night the day,
Thou canst not then be false to any man.
                              —William Shakespeare

Every one of us makes mistakes and harms others at times. In almost every interaction we have with another person, there is the potential for misunderstanding or manipulation. After examining our past, we must have the personal integrity to admit our mistakes. Covering them up only leads to internal pain, increasing our feeling of shame, and guaranteeing that we will repeat the very actions that got us in trouble in the first place.

Many of us feel relief after admitting our past errors quietly to God and to ourselves, but this is usually as far as we want to go. It's not enough to get us the way to happiness, though. To break old patterns, we must tell our past to another person who can listen objectively. This frees us from the isolation that men so often fall into, especially when we feel vulnerable to criticism. We see that our past behavior has been less than perfect and, naturally, we regret it. But to avoid the pain of hiding from others, trying to keep our secrets under lock and key, we must speak freely (to someone trustworthy) about these faults and mistakes. Doing so cleanses the soul and uplifts the spirit.

Today I have the integrity to shine the light of Truth on my past and to tell another human being my personal history, both the good and the bad.

166. The Spiritual Principle of Willingness

Nothing is impossible to a willing heart.
—John Heywood

Am I really willing to have all of my faults, seen and unseen, removed? Isn't there a hidden part of myself, destructive though it may be, that I hold on to, just in case I need it? Revenge, or self-pity, for example. Or an attraction to pathos. We each have a hidden side, a darker aspect of our nature that we don't usually reveal until we're angry or resentful. Then we start brooding, and the dark gets darker. This aspect of myself is something I have clung to because I think I'd disappear or be powerless without it.

I need willingness to look deep inside my psyche, be ready to let go of anything in me that stands in the way of aligning my will with that of my Higher Power. This spiritual willingness is an awesome commitment. I am being asked to surrender my limited vision of myself, and to be transformed by grace. It means giving up who I thought I was, in order to become who I truly am. In many ways, this idea of letting go of myself is incomprehensible. Nevertheless, I can strive for the willingness to be transformed; this is all that is necessary.

Today I am willing to look at all of who I am.

JUNE 15

There is no humiliation in humility.
—Joseph Roux

By asking our Creator to remove our shortcomings, we admit that through self-will alone we cannot heal ourselves. This opens the door to humility. Throughout our lives we were taught to be self-reliant, never asking for anything. Now we ask for help. By acknowledging that "I can't" and "God can," we begin to learn the true meaning of humility.

Again and again we have tried to "go it alone," only to find each time that we couldn't make any real progress without tapping into a spiritual force. There is no humiliation in this knowledge. Instead there is hope and joy in humbly knowing that our Creator is both wiser and more powerful than we are and, if asked, will actively help us on our journey.

Today I will humbly ask my Creator to guide me on my journey.

168. The Spiritual Principle of Brotherly Love

Love is all we have, the only way that each can help the other.

—Euripides

Listing all of the people I've harmed, and becoming willing to make amends for my actions, is a task that I prefer to avoid. However, accepting responsibility for my behavior, becoming accountable to the people I hurt, frees me from my past and opens up a whole new way of being with others. Only by becoming willing to make amends do I begin to realize how my own behavior has isolated me from others. Isolation and estrangement are outgrowths of fear and guilt. But these phantoms disappear when I become willing to seek out those I've hurt, in order to set things right.

Then I begin to experience brotherly love. Love through action is a powerful form of healing that mends both my internal hurts *and* the harm I have done to others. My willingness to take action to redress my wrongs demonstrates that I am ready and able to experience a greater love.

Today, by becoming willing to right a wrong I have done to another, I will invite the experience of brotherly love into my life.

169. The Spiritual Principle of Discipline

I am, indeed, a king, because I know how to rule myself.

—Pietro Aretino

In spite of my fear, guilt feelings, shame, and self-righteous anger, I seek out those I have harmed and attempt to make amends for my actions. This requires tremendous self-discipline. It would be so much easier just to pretend the past didn't happen and then move on with my life. It would be simpler to believe that it wouldn't do any good to face people with the truth of my behavior. But this kind of rationalization is a trick played by my old thinking patterns. The fact is, if I don't come to terms with my past errors, they will live in my body as a pocket of fear, and in this form they will continue to maintain control over me and my choices.

Discipline gives me the resolve not to take the easy way out, but to confront the past with courage, and to make a sincere effort to heal the injury I have caused. Taking this direct action brings with it a tremendous freedom. No longer will fear of discovery, guilt, and shame rule my actions. I am able to face the world with a clean slate and a joyful heart.

Today I will make amends directly to someone I have harmed.

170. The Spiritual Principle of Perseverance

The person who makes a success of living is the one who sees his goal steadily and aims for it unswervingly. That is dedication.
—Cecil B. De Mille

Through the application of the first nine spiritual principles, I have dealt with my past. But, by itself, just cleaning up the past isn't enough to help me build a wonderful future. On a daily basis, I must continue to review my choices and my motives. This is called self-inquiry, or spiritual self-examination. Were I to neglect this continuing inner work, I would run the risk of committing the same errors over and over again.

To stay determined to examine my life requires great perseverance. Many little activities and concerns can get in the way. I may be extremely busy in my work, relationships, or other life commitments. However, when I do not persist in looking squarely at my actions and addressing my mistakes, I will eventually fall back into old self-destructive patterns. Continual self-inquiry keeps my life simple and free of fear.

Today I shall persist in reviewing my actions and making amends if necessary.

JUNE 19

If thou may not continually gather thyself together, do it sometime at least once a day, morning or evening.

—Thomas à Kempis

Spiritual awareness is the foundation of positive, creative change in my life. It is crucial that I continue my spiritual development, for without it I stagnate and eventually become self-destructive. Spiritual awareness is no accident; it requires work and commitment. A daily plan of action that includes prayer and meditation is the most effective method to assure my continued spiritual growth. Each of us must work out his own form of prayer and meditation. Whatever the form, we must *keep doing it.* After tasting the incredible soul-food of regular spiritual practice, I will wonder how I lived for so long without it.

Paying lip service to this principle yields very little. At this point in my progress, if I desire full recovery, then nothing less than a lifelong commitment to these principles will satisfy me. If one day at a time I seek awareness through prayer and meditation, my Higher Power will do the rest.

Today, in my own way, I will pray and meditate.

172. The Spiritual Principle of Service

JUNE 20

*The noblest service comes from nameless
    hands,*
And the best servant does his work unseen.
        —Oliver Wendell Holmes

Service is the guiding spiritual principle
that connects us to each other. Without a
commitment to serve, my life would be
consumed with self-centeredness and
petty desires. Service gives me the opportunity to reach out beyond myself and
give to others. Putting this principle into
action, I share with my community the
same gift of caring and compassion that I
have received from my Higher Power. The
message I bring is often the simple offering of love, of lightheartedness, of listening well.

As I seize these opportunities, I find
that my life makes a difference in the lives
of others. Each person I touch in the spirit
of service will touch the lives of others.
Through this ever-widening circle of service, our community, our nation, the entire world can be transformed into a more
humane and loving place.

*Today I will be of service to another human
being.*

173. Summer

Summer play . . . is likely to mean exploring. . . . As far down the evolutionary scale as some fishes, there is a summer urge to venture into new waters, and many species of birds and mammals wander about for no known reasons except to satisfy curiosity.
—Sally Carrighar

Today is the summer solstice, the official beginning of summer. Ah, it is about time. Summer is a time of play, even for creatures other than humans, it appears. Summer seems to go by so fast. Suddenly it is over. Summer is when things grow. Watching plants grow can be joyous and can heighten the sense of the mystery of life.

In humans and in some animals, summer can trigger curiosity and the urge to explore. When these are blocked in a man, he is diminished. Giving vent to our urge to wander about and see things is important. Do you remember a particularly joyous summer? Perhaps you went on a great vacation. Or had some great playmates one summer. Remember that summer, bringing it to mind when you want to increase your joy.

Today I will be curious, exploring and playing, in the spirit of summer.

174. Burning Beauty

Nothing can live or grow without warmth, yet nothing can destroy like fire.
                    —Dorothy MacLean

The sun enlivens and nurtures with its power. Its burning beauty is fierce, and untouchable. "Do not get too close" is the sun's clear message; "protect yourself." In Greek mythology Icarus ignored this message; his wax wings melted and he plummeted to his death.

Some people possess a burning beauty; we learn to admire them from a distance. Others radiate a beauty that is less intense but no less vital, like the flame that burns in our hearts. These people draw us toward them, almost as if to say "Touch me." Both forms of beauty can sustain us; learning to recognize the difference is key.

Today I will look to see beauty in various forms —male and female, cold and hot, young and old. I will remember, too, that which gives life can also take it away.

175. Come Away!

Come away, O human child!
To the waters and the wild
With a faery, hand in hand,
For the world's more full of weeping than
*   you can understand.*
                              —William Butler Yeats

"Come away," the great Irish poet Yeats beckoned. Many men today are responding to his call. We are learning to address the boy within each man, calling him away from passivity, addiction, self-hatred, and violence. We call him to "the waters and the wild"—a fresh place where things can grow and change. The journey there may be long and full of obstacles, but there is much joy along the way.

Having a guide is essential, as are intimacy and trust. The guide may be half your size. That is what Yeats meant by "faery," a metaphor for the magician, one who can transform the mundane into the sacred. One must go in the body—"hand in hand"—to this other world. The journey will not always be easy; weeping is inevitable. As we get more comfortable, relaxed, and vulnerable, feeling safe, we are likely to release feelings that we have been holding on to.

Where would the "waters and the wild" be for you? How might you get there?

176. Forgiveness

In order to derive strength from God and the angels, it is necessary to enter into active contact with them, to push against them with our muscles and feel them with our senses. We are formed not by abstract laws but by the intimacies of a wrestling match.

—Deane Juhan

We have experienced many wrongs in our lives. Many of us were hurt and abandoned as boys. As young men, we were prepared for war. We were lied to about what would be important for our happiness. We have been beaten up, both physically and emotionally. How can we grant forgiveness to those who wounded us?

True forgiveness is not an isolated act. It is a natural part of the greater process of self-examination and exploration that we are engaged in daily. As we work out the wounds of the past, forgiveness will one day come easily. We do not need to work at it. If we try to forgive while we still feel angry and resentful, we will only repress our pain and hurt ourselves. As we grow in awareness, real forgiveness comes as an unexpected gift.

Today I will let go of forgiveness as a goal and allow my inner process to unfold without expectations.

177. Mentors

When love and skill work together, expect a masterpiece.

—John Ruskin

It is not always easy for us to ask for guidance and direction. Early on, we learned that self-sufficiency and remoteness were "manly" characteristics. Without direction and the shared experience of other, older men, we may make many mistakes in life that might have been avoided.

A mentor is someone who shares his wisdom and knowledge. Hearing about his triumphs and mistakes helps us keep things in perspective. A mentor does not run our life for us, but he can help us set a course through the obstacles that appear on our path.

Today I give up being lost and alone. I will look for someone who can share his experience, strength, and hope with me, who can offer guidance and love.

178. Change

Life is not orderly. No matter how we try to make life so, right in the middle of it we die, lose a leg, fall in love, drop a jar of applesauce.
—Natalie Goldberg

Everything changes. Change is a constant in life. Change often happens without our permission. Change is a key aspect of masculinity. But too many of us, forgetting that fact, have frozen our images of what it means to be a man. One's masculinity does not have to be once and for all. We learn how to be men from various sources —fathers, teachers, coaches, uncles, friends, and many others. Women can also help teach us what it means to be a man. As we grow and as the world changes, our masculinity can mature. As we confront obstacles, ordeals, and joys in life, our masculinity can emerge.

Becoming a man is not an event; it is a lifelong process. Our manhood is determined by a variety of inside factors that emerge and outside factors that influence us. A single event—birth, marriage, the death of another—can radically change a man's life and his sense of himself. Only by staying open to change can we fully become men.

How do I respond to change when it comes my way, unsolicited? Is there something I would like to change? How might I go about making the changes I want? Is there someone who can help me? Are there things changing in my life that I need to accept?

179. Contrary Demands

At a time when women, with good reason, are asking men to make known their most guarded feelings, when we want them to love and raise babies and remember our birthdays, it is also required that they be the ones to rescue people in a burning building. And startle the dragons when they are heard in the dark.

—Gloria Emerson

Contrary demands placed upon men make life confusing. Sometimes we put those demands on ourselves. Or they come from friends and loved ones. This double bind can be virtually impossible to resolve. If a man is not guided by an inner masculine core, he may find himself subject to multiple demands and whims. The cross fire of demands from others can lead to passivity, violence, and even suicide.

Men benefit from developing and following their own agendas, rather than those of parents, spouses, children, bosses. It is important to listen to others, but we must not allow their needs and ideas to drown out our own inner voices. Despite those who claim it is "a man's world," there are many "nice guys" who have difficulty first deciding what they want and then actively pursuing it. Being aware of, acknowledging, and naming contrary demands in one's life can be important steps toward resolving them.

Am I experiencing any contrary demands in my life right now? Am I pulled in more than one direction? Today I will allow my imagination to conceive of a way for these demands to be resolved.

180. Spirituality

It is easy enough to drive the spirit out of the door, but when we have done so the salt of life grows flat—it loses its savour.

—Carl G. Jung

Life can become so busy. The day-to-day tasks at work, with family, even the time required just to care for myself, can push my spiritual needs into the background. Sometimes it seems there isn't enough time to do everything, as though the pressures of life will overcome me. When I'm in this state, the world looks terrible. Life becomes flat and humdrum, or frantic and frightening.

If I pause to focus on my spiritual condition and what I need to become more aware, a funny thing happens. I begin to enjoy myself and my life more. Each task seems to carry a magical rhythm of its own that I can follow. Time becomes a friend, and the daily business of living flows effortlessly. The time I spend in meditation and prayer adds to my day rather than taking away from it. When I remove myself briefly from the rush to "get things done," my life takes on richness and color.

Today I will spend some time in a state of surrender, in prayer or meditation or contemplation. In this way, I recharge myself inwardly, freeing up my energy to live with joy.

181. Selfless Service

For whom shall we build a throne of soft cushions? For our own vanity's sake, thinking that we are better than others? No, for the pleasure of others, and not for our vanity.
— Hazrat Inayat Khan

It is so easy to get caught up in my worries, my goals, my desires, so that the world begins to seem full of pressure and turmoil. From all sides I hear, "You need this car, that job, this trip, that house," and on and on, ad infinitum. The pressure to need, to gather up more and more "stuff," to be self-involved, can be very real. The more "things" I acquire, the more I want. Yet, just as the wise ones have repeatedly explained, nothing outside me brings lasting satisfaction.

Right now is the time to break this cycle of self-centeredness, to move from "I need" to "I offer," to serve humanity rather than focusing on what I can get for myself. I can do this by creating kindness and beauty around me. I can smile at a salesclerk, spend time with a child, lend a hand to someone in need. The opportunities to spread goodwill are boundless. All I "need" is to be willing to serve; then I will find that blessings and miracles naturally flow into my life in great abundance. The secret, and the joy, of this kind of wealth is to serve without thought of reward.

As I walk through the world today, I will be aware of the opportunities given to me to create beauty and kindness.

182. Pausing

Sometimes, when a bird cries out,
Or the wind sweeps through a tree,
Or a dog howls on a far off farm,
I hold still and listen a long time.
> —Hermann Hesse, (translated by
> Robert Bly)

Pausing can literally extend your life, especially in this too-fast world where people zip along too rapidly. They can kill themselves, or us. So take a break. Slow down. Pause.

A lot of speedy city guys come to some men's gatherings. They are encouraged to slow down. Certain types of games help them to slow down, such as making them go through an obstacle course before getting into the dining area. Don't rush your food down! Life is not the military.

Pauses can be among our most memorable moments—to see a bird lift off in flight, to hear a coyote howl at night, to linger at a meal. In our fast-moving society it is essential to take time to pause. The spaces in between are what make great poetry, knowing when to breathe. When a dancer pauses, all the beauty of his body and its movement can be clear.

Today I will take the time to pause, even if it means being late to something. I can pause on my way somewhere, perhaps seeing some things for the first time, like trees or flowers that I have never noticed before.

183. Midlife: A New Birth

JULY 1

It may be that when we no longer know what to do we have come to our real work and that when we no longer know which way to go we have begun our real journey.
—Wendell Berry

At midlife, many men feel lost, confused, uncertain of the terrain ahead. We turn to look back at the more familiar past, and we know we can't bring the old ways forward into the future with us. The second half of life calls for a kind of rebirth.

We don't have to leave our career or our spouse in order to meet this challenge, but we can take stock of how we work and relate to others. We can understand ourselves differently in the world. We can take the pressure off ourselves to prove our worth through work, since we know now that we're worthwhile regardless of what work we do.

Creating small changes to meet our changing lives is our *real* work. Becoming new men inside, getting a clearer understanding of life's priorities, is the road our changing body and soul must walk. We can no longer coast on the blissful ignorance of youth; now we must roll up our sleeves and use our great inner resources —wisdom, faith, love—to live the rest of our lives as honorably as we can.

Today I'll admit to myself and to another man that I'm a little scared and uncertain about the changes in my life. I'll admit, too, that I'm a little excited about the possibility of experiencing the mysteries in life that still lie ahead.

184. Depression

The contemporary male increasingly experiences uncertainty, depression, dependency, loneliness, despair.

—Jerome Bernstein

Some men get lost, particularly in midlife, and enter a depression from which they may never recover. Strategies for dealing with depression include physical activity, starting something new, joining a men's group, going to a men's gathering, creating something artistic. Expressing sadness or anger can help release us from depression. Even having a good fight with members of a men's group who can contain that energy and not be destroyed by it can help a man move through depression. Expressed conflict that is authentic, especially if there is agreement to preserve the relationship, can reduce depression.

Sometimes we think that we are the only ones with a certain feeling. This can isolate us from others, perhaps in the belief that they will not understand. The expression of that feeling can have the reverse effect—connecting us to others who may be experiencing or have experienced the same feeling.

How do I typically deal with depression? Is that strategy adequate? Perhaps today is a good time to try another approach.

185. Self-Encouragement

*Every man in the world is better than
    someone else.
And not as good as someone else.*
                                —William Saroyan

"Good work!" These are words many of
us seldom heard as boys. As men, we may
still feel awkward giving or receiving
praise, even when that praise is honest
and well deserved. Most important, we
recognize a great need *to tell ourselves*
when we're doing well.

We are doing good work, not just on
the job, or in the garden, or in the home,
but in our lives. That good inner work—
getting through past wounds, breaking
unworkable patterns—is keeping us
strong, sober, and sane: in fact, this
strength, sobriety, and sanity are what allow us to admit that we had become weak,
drunk, and insane in the first place. The
work we do makes us strong enough to
accept help from a friend, to share in a
support group, to call, if we choose, on a
Higher Power.

*I have worked hard to face both the demons of
fear and the angels of grace that life has pre-
sented to me. Today I will say to myself, "Good
work!"—and I will mean it.*

186. Freedom and Commitment

JULY 4

Everyone is in the best seat.

—John Cage

We spend a lot of time and energy struggling between our commitments to family, friends, and work, and our desire to be free and "unattached." At times it feels as if a great weight presses down on our shoulders, as though we're bound too tightly by our chosen responsibilities. Then we sometimes escape into fantasy, longing to sail alone into the sunset or become a nomad moving from place to place without answering to anyone.

Then we remember a child running up to say, "Look at this!" when he has discovered something new and wonderful. We recall the times our partners come up and hug us for no reason except that they love us. Or a friend calls just to tell us that we are appreciated and loved. These are only a few of the rewards we are continually receiving, the natural result of the different commitments we have made.

I am free. I choose the kind of life I live, and I choose to love my life.

187. Men's Feelings

Men often enter genuine feeling for the first time when in deep grief, after cheerfulness and excitement have failed for years to bring them there.

—Robert Bly

Men feel, very deeply. If you ever have any doubt, look at the music and art that Mozart, Picasso, and other men have created to express feelings—our individual ones, those of our gender, and those on behalf of all people. Men have much to be proud of with respect to feelings. The diversity of our feelings, many of which we do not yet have words for, is considerable.

Men sometimes lack the words to express feelings. This does not mean that we are without feelings or that our feelings lack importance, simply that their expression in a verbal form may not be immediately forthcoming. Sometimes a man turns to something physical or artistic, rather than verbal, to communicate. It is important for men to avoid using feminine guidelines for feelings. Men can learn from women, certainly, and in many ways the sexes are alike. But in some areas, such as feelings and their expression, we can be quite different. We need not judge ourselves harshly if we are not fluent in the language of feelings.

How might I express my feelings today in a way that is appropriate to who I am?

188. Heroes

When John Wayne rode through my childhood, and perhaps through yours, he determined forever the shape of certain dreams.
—Joan Didion

So what's wrong with John Wayne? He was a good guy, strong, a protector. Sometimes people say, "Don't be a John Wayne." Why not? Of course, we don't necessarily want to *be* John Wayne, but he portrayed many male characteristics that are worthy of admiration.

Sure, he didn't cry a lot. But neither do most of us. We may cry sometimes; sometimes we feel sad without tears. The character John Wayne played was often fiercely protective. The paternal part of us appreciates that. John Wayne portrayed men who were larger than life, who embodied courage, honor, loyalty, and compassion. He was a celluloid hero, and that's okay. We know the difference between the movies and reality. And we can still like John Wayne.

Today I will enjoy my manliness in all of its many forms.

189. Male Beauty

By the end of the (men's) weekend I am deeply struck by the many forms of male beauty: Big roaring bears of men, fierce flying falcons of men, deep diving trout of men. Gentle men, angry men, laughing men . . . men hugging, men howling, crying, men dancing, singing. . . .

—Terrance O'Connor

Men can be so beautiful—to see, to watch, to hear—their bodies, voices, ways of being and thinking. Many men notice only women; some men are becoming freer to notice men to whom we are drawn. It may be the way they walk. Or the clarity in what they say. Or their dignity. Or the sound of their voices. Men singing together can be particularly beautiful. There is much to admire in men. Men are many things that are simply beautiful. And we do many things that are beautiful—in our relationships to ourselves, to others, to nature, and to the divine.

Today I will take the time to notice and admire men's beauty.

190. The Art of Manhood

Storytelling, drumming, dancing, and singing are practical during the dry season.
                                    —Malidoma Some

Our "dry periods" are a great time to revive in ourselves the art of storytelling, the drama to be found in dance, the delight of drumming, and the salvation that singing can provide. All this did not die in our boyhood—it can be part of our life again.

We tend to let professional performers have all the fun. In doing so, we become less inclined to create this kind of magic on our own. We may still carry old voices inside that tell us we can't sing, that we're not artistically inclined, or that storytellers are born, not made. We challenge those voices today by doing the forbidden thing: allowing our joy and our grief all manner of expression.

Men are now reclaiming their ancient abilities in the arts. We are healing ourselves and others in the process, building a new kind of beauty to leave behind. By reaching deep into ourselves through drum and dance, through story and song, we reawaken the colorful qualities of manhood.

Today I'll tell a story, whether it's ancient or one of my own. I'll drum out the storm that's rumbling in my soul. I'll dance out the demons that tell me I can't dance. I'll sing in delight, knowing that joy's melody is always in the perfect key.

191. Old Male Friends

A person begins his spiritual accomplishment by learning how to be a friend.
                        —Hazrat Inayat Khan

These men knew me before I knew myself. They loved me when I felt unlovable. They showed their affection as best they could, whether by loaning me a few bucks, buying me a beer, or grabbing me around the neck and tackling me. They connected with me in the only ways they knew.

It's important to appreciate these guys, to remember and reach out to them —through a phone call, a letter, or by dropping by when I'm in the neighborhood.

My new friends know and love me *now*, in my recovery and my sanity. But the old ones are to be treasured and valued, too. They loved me *then*, when I saw nothing lovable in myself.

Today I can contact an old male friend, directly or simply in my heart, to say, "Thanks for your love."

192. Manly Hugs

JULY 10

Man is free, but not if he doesn't believe it.
—Giovanni Giacomo Casanova

As we grew up, many of us were not at all encouraged to show our affection for the men who were important to us. Occasionally we could hug our fathers or our grandfathers. But after a point, usually when we were about eight years old, even this limited kind of manly contact was forbidden. As a result of this "hugging taboo," we became physically isolated from other men. We could touch each other in the simulated combat of team sports, or in a fit of drunken sentiment, but we were taught that to touch a man with genuine affection or feeling seemed somehow "unmanly."

Now we recognize the hunger we have for the nurturing touch of other men. Being hugged by another man is a greatly supportive and empowering experience. Reaching out to hug another man, we share the physical expression of our manliness. When we hug, we are vulnerable. We need to experience hugs with other men. We are nurturers, and we can be nurtured.

Today I will receive and give hugs in a respectful and loving way.

193. Wildness and Wild Men

JULY 11

*In Wildness is the preservation of the World.
. . . I would have every man so much like a
wild antelope, so much a part and parcel of
nature. . . . The most alive is the wildest.*
—Henry David Thoreau

"All good things are wild and free," according to Thoreau. "Give me for my friends and neighbors, wild men, not tame ones." We are blessed if we have friends who are truly wild men. Wild here does not mean those who drink heavily or hurt people. It means those unpredictable ones who might bring wild gifts, invite us on forays into nature, and refresh our souls in a multitude of ways. We never know what our wild friends will do or when they may appear. They can be embarrassing. Their clothing can be unusual. They can bring us great delight and joy. When men lose touch with the wilderness, they lose contact with an essential part of their masculinity. Outer wildness can evoke our natural wildness—that which is spontaneous, alive, zany, and fresh.

Remember a time when you had direct contact with natural wildness. Imagine it or literally go out and find some wildness. Be wild enough to cancel any tame regular plans and go off into a wilderness.

194. I Am a Part of All Life

The windows of my soul I throw
Wide open to the sun.
                    —John Greenleaf Whittier

This day I remember that I am part of a
wonderful gathering. When I open my
eyes to all life, the rocks, flowers, birds,
animals, and human beings seem to leap
out of the shadows and into a place of harmony, of belonging. Seeing the world in
this way, I want to experience everything
and everyone! I want to take in the distinc-
tive sound, color, and fragrance of each
one of us, delighting in our differences
that fill this life with mystery, marveling
at our endless variety. All around me,
above and below me, this earth is teeming
with life, seen and unseen.

In the past I tended to keep to myself
or to hide away with a select few others. I
know it's all right to cherish being alone at
times. But today I'm letting more of life
touch me. Both solitude and community
are necessary to the growth of the soul.

Today I feel a part of all that is: the creatures of
the world, the people and places, and their end-
less energy and beauty. The whole world is my
home today, and I trust it.

195. Birds, Wings, and Flying

The reason why birds can fly and we can't is simply that they have perfect faith, for to have faith is to have wings.

—James M. Barrie

Birds, and especially their wings, can be so beautiful, so functional, so effective. You may want to walk outside so you can see a bird fly. Note how effortlessly it moves its wings. How skillfully it sails through the air.

Perhaps you will be lucky enough to see a group of birds flying together. Certain kinds of birds, such as geese, have mastered the art of teamwork. They are quite efficient and know how to fly in patterns that maximize their efficiency. They also can teach us how to share leadership. When the lead bird, who takes most of the wind's assault, gets tired, he simply moves to the rear and another bird takes over. This sharing of leadership is a good idea, much better than competing for leadership. It allows for rest and a time to gather strength.

Birds in flight have a unique beauty. We can learn from birds.

196. Cactus Wisdom

The cactus of the high desert is a small, grubby, obscure and humble vegetable. Yet from this nest of thorns, this snare of hooks and fiery spines, is born once each year a splendid flower . . . soft, lovely, sweet, desirable, exemplifying better than the rose among thorns the unity of opposites.
—Edward Abbey

Every plant has its own wisdom and hence something to teach men. The giant saguaro cacti, stately creatures of the Southwestern desert, are instructive. They stand firm, a quality that is important for men to embody. They also teach us how to set boundaries and keep out unwelcome energies and influences. Some people invade boundaries and need to be held off. Their energy can drain us, leaving us exhausted. When such a person comes toward us, it is good to have internalized the strength and resolve of the cactus, which learns to survive in a difficult environment without losing dignity. The saguaro also teaches us to reach high. Its flowers and fruits can be quite beautiful, shining in the desert.

We humans are quite diverse; we can move from being cactuslike, keeping things out, to being spongelike, and absorbing. We have many potentialities within us. Learning the properties of various plants and animals and knowing when to assume them can be valuable. At times we need to be pointed, a task with which the cactus can assist us. The wisdom of the cactus is considerable and unique.

Knowledge of the natural external world can enrich our natural internal world.

197. Claiming My Life

You can never have a greater or a lesser dominion than that over yourself.
—Leonardo da Vinci

I claim the right to all the gold I've found in the hills of my soul. I stake claim on all the jewels I've found in my valleys. I claim the right to walk through the forests of my forgotten childhood, and am determined to come out on the other side richer in spirit than when I went in.

I claim responsibility for my mistakes, as well as for my achievements. I claim myself, declaring independence from father, mother, factory, coworkers, the products I help to create, and all the processes and institutions that would enslave me.

What a paradox, that claiming myself gives me the strength to understand my family and community as mine, and to love fearlessly, from the center of my soul.

Today I claim my sovereignty as a unique person with unique gifts.

198. Men and Community

With the breakdown of the community of men, we no longer have access to relationships that restore a feeling of connectedness and belonging.

—Francis Weller

Before the Industrial Revolution, men would gather to harvest food, raise barns, and volunteer to fight fires. Men used to help each other in many ways; men banded together for mutual aid. With the rise of industrialism, living and working became more separate and isolated. Cooperative masculinities are less prevalent today than they were in the earlier days of America. We have lost a lot. Neighborhoods have broken up and work units have become more fragmented. The community of men has been badly damaged.

In recent years men's communities have been reemerging. In community each man can contribute his own strengths and be supported in areas where he is less developed. Strengthening communities of men can help with mixed communities of men and women and of men, women, and children. When men join men's groups, they are likely to communicate better and function easier in other groups, such as in families and at work.

What community or communities am I a part of? If I am not part of a community, how can I help build such a community today? If I am part of one, what can I do today to strengthen this community?

199. The Other Side of Control

We find comfort among those who agree with us—growth among those who don't.
—Frank A. Clark

As we heal, we come to learn that we really can't control others, that we have to stop trying to get other people to change. It takes awhile, but gradually we're starting to understand and benefit from this simple truth.

Some of us have yet to consider the defeatist attitude that underlies the desire to control, that part of us that says: "She's always been that way. She's never going to change," or "What I hoped for is never going to happen." This is plain old negative thinking, a mental habit that can fool us into trying to fix things by controlling events. Such "stuck thinking" causes us to react in the same way over and over again.

Everybody and everything is changing all the time. Why do we sometimes believe that it isn't? Maybe the uncertain boy in us is still thinking in magical terms: if he could only apply a certain technique, say the magic word, act a certain way, maybe he could keep from getting hurt or disappointed. We don't have to punish that kid. Instead we can gently explain to him that things don't always work that way.

Today I'll witness the ways I try to predict and control the behavior of others. I'll reassure the little boy inside me that we'll have much more fun letting life unfold as a good mystery should.

200. Wandering

Only those who will risk going too far can possibly find out how far one can go.
—T. S. Eliot

Many men spend years, decades, wandering the inner wilderness searching for the water that would quench their soul-thirst, looking for a place to call home, hoping for help, praying for a miracle. Now we are discovering that there are places where the wanderer in us can rest, take nourishment, and receive nurturing. Men are now creating such places at last, and others are finding them.

For some, that place will be a men's group; for others, a Twelve Step meeting, or simply the home of a friend. When a confused and weary wanderer appears at our door, we must remember what it was like for us the first time we came in out of the cold, walking into arms that we barely trusted. We must remember how we feared rejection. We must remember how alone it felt, to be wandering.

Help is here. Hope is here. The miracle is in the making—in the men who are meeting together to laugh, drum, dance, grieve, and heal, to write a new story of manhood. Men are nourishing and nurturing each other, and all the wanderers are welcome.

Today I'll remember. If I'm still wandering I'll walk into a room full of men somewhere, to try to find a home for a soul and a body tired of roving the world alone.

201. Back to the Source

Where is the love, beauty and truth we seek,
But in our mind?
                                —Percy Bysshe Shelley

Sometimes I just can't figure things out. I feel out of control, perplexed, out of sorts. Then I'll hear a song on the radio, or see something beautiful that reminds me of what I love, or hear the call of a certain bird that flies me right back into childhood. Just taking a walk at these times reminds me there is no such thing as distance, no such state as "all alone."

Before leaving for work, during a break in the day's schedule, just before going to sleep, I'm going to remember those moments of connectedness—seeing a fine picture, reading a great poem, appreciating a model airplane, an old TV show, a good song. Absorbing these small pleasures takes me back to the source of all beauty, energy, and bliss. As I remember what lifts me up, I'll let myself feel uplifted; I'll rest in that fullness and walk in that knowledge.

Today I'll seek out that which is truly beautiful, the source that connects me to what is real and meaningful in my life.

202. Weeping

Weeping . . . softens the hardened and dried-out soul, making it receptive and alive. It clears the mind. It opens the heart. Tears soften, clarify, and open.

—Alan Jones

"Big boys don't cry" is a spell cast on many male children. Such a spell prevents them from drawing on a natural healing process. "Stiff upper lip" is a common cover-up in the face of pain and loss. Or "If you don't stop crying, I'll give you something to cry about." Did you have these or similar spells cast on you while growing up? To break their curse, it helps to remember the exact words and any gesture that came with them. Then we can work to erase these restrictive messages and create new ones that give us permission to weep.

Telling a child not to cry can bind shame to weeping. The child will learn to feel that there is something inherently wrong and shameful with crying. Grown men can benefit from shame reduction to enable ourselves to cry again. We can relearn how to cry. Too many adults forget the natural healing waters and benefits that flow when we release the dams. Warriors of old wept openly at the loss of comrades. Weeping is manly. Cutting off tears disables a man's healing. Tears are a sign of healing, an indication that the body is restoring itself. Tears are a great mystery that serve to cleanse.

Perhaps there are tears I have been holding on to. If so, today might be a good day to release them.

203. Lighten Up

Angels can fly because they take themselves lightly.

—G. K. Chesterton

A lot of men tend to take themselves seriously. Their furrowed brows say to everyone, "Don't worry, I'm worrying about it." We have only one pair of shoulders, but sometimes we try to carry the weight of the whole world. So how do we keep from getting old before our time? How do we keep from seeing everything with tired eyes?

By finding and befriending that boy inside us, we learn to lighten up a bit. By releasing the weight of his hurts, his sadness and anger, we become lighter. By taking that little boy out to play and giving him plenty of rest, the heart is free to soar and so is the imagination. The creativity of this inner boy can turn responsibilities into games, and burdens into honors.

Today I'll fly with the angels—I'll play, relax, rest, read, walk, talk, beat a drum.

204. Creating

Keep on sowing your seed, for you never know which will grow—perhaps it all will.

—Ecclesiastes 11:6

Many of us men have been taught to see ourselves as "destroyers." The truth is that men are *both* creators and destroyers. Both states exist in us, making perfect balance possible. So often we have felt that our life is being taken apart piece by piece, then put back together again in an entirely new way. Like Kali—the aspect of God that causes both creation and annihilation —life moves and changes according to this divine balance. It may look hectic to us at times, but there is perfection in it.

Some of us fall out of balance for a long time. We stay in touch with the part of ourselves that can bulldoze, level, and clear-cut. But we grow out of touch with the creative fellow in us, the one who has incredible ideas and the ability to see them through to fruition.

It takes much more time to create than it does to destroy. The time, patience, and permission needed to generate something from nothing has been granted to the "artists" among us. We must give ourselves this kind of time, for in renewing our creativity, we renew and re-create ourselves.

Today I will honor the One in myself who loves to make things new. Today nothing will stop me from creating something—a poem, a possibility, a story, a simple song, a new vision of relationship, a new feeling of hope for this world.

205. How Young Is Old?

How old would you be if you didn't know how old you was?

—Satchel Paige

An eighty-six-year-young man rides his bicycle to work every day. A thirty-five-year-old man is depressed because he feels his life is over. We all know people who refuse to yield to time, and those who throw in the towel prematurely. Many of us see pictures of our fathers and men of their generation looking gray and brittle at age forty! That "look" has nothing to do with chronological age.

Choosing the honorable life, being true to our dreams, eating healthful food, keeping good company, giving and receiving support and nurturance: all these keep the flame burning in the belly, and the spark alight in the eye.

Today I'll examine the quality, not the number, of my years.

206. Looking to a Higher Power

Whatever satisfies the soul is truth.
                                    —Walt Whitman

In the still, dark morning, I feel the loving quiet of a Higher Power. On mornings like this I remember that lying next to the one I love can't bring me serenity, nor can my work or my bank account.

This peace I feel comes from deep within me, from a place perfect in silence, perfect in love. Part of me is always at peace. From that place comes my strength and goodness. I go there, and am humbled. I go there, and am filled with a powerful joy.

Today, drawing in the deep gift of breath, I let out a strong sigh. It is a sign of strength to love God. I look to a Higher Power for peace and serenity.

207. Self-Discovery

I have come to feel that the only learning which significantly influences behavior is self-discovered, self-appropriated learning.
                                    —Carl R. Rogers

I can only learn so much by reading, or by listening to others. The real truths, the ones that stay with me, are found when I look inward, asking the deepest questions of myself. These are the answers that truly mean something to me, that give me a sense of self-direction and self-mastery. My inner questions don't need to be complicated ones. There is a great value in simply asking myself, "Who am I?"

Today I can reflect upon who I am by answering these four open-ended questions. Writing down my answers will enable me to review them over the next few days, to look for changes.

> *Today I am . . .*
> *Today I feel . . .*
> *Today I think . . .*
> *Today I wish . . .*

208. Solitude and Strength

Every moment and every event of every man's life on earth plants something in his soul. For just as the wind carries thousands of winged seeds, so each moment brings with it germs of spiritual vitality.

—Thomas Merton

Many years ago a man went on a solitary canoe trip into the forest of northeastern Canada. He did not begin his trip alone, but one by one his friends left for home. He decided to stay. For days he was completely isolated from other human beings. His companions were the swift rivers, the open sky, the ground that spoke where his feet landed. There were bears. One day, caught in a storm on the lake, he paddled for hours, fighting wind and strong current, before he reached a dry bank where he could rest. That day on the water, he found a strength inside himself that he had never known before.

Standing there exhausted, he watched the continuing fury of the water and wind. He was humbled by their power. He had used nearly all his physical and mental energy to get his canoe to the bank, but he knew that a greater strength than his had brought him to safety.

Today I acknowledge the inner strength I possess. I honor the Higher Power that can also be known through the wind and water, the Power that sustains the life and growth of every creature on Earth, including me.

209. Choices

When you have to make a choice and don't make it, that is in itself a choice.
　　　　　　　　　　　—William James

Today we have a choice about how we live our lives. For many years, driven by fear, addictions, pride, and a host of other forces that seemed beyond our control, we may have felt as if we had no choice. Every day was just like every other day; our internal awareness was frozen behind a curtain of delusion and self-doubt.

The curtain begins to lift when we become willing to admit we are powerless over our fears and addictions, that we must surrender our illusion of control. Then we enter a strange and wonderful world of paradox where we "surrender to win" and "let go" to gain control. None of it makes any sense, and yet it works! When we struggle with choices, those who have learned to live comfortably in this paradoxical world chuckle and remind us to "relax and let go." When we do, our choices seem to make themselves. For the first time in our lives, we are at ease.

Today I will make some choices, but I will also let some choices make themselves—not through lethargy, but through consciously relaxing and letting go.

210. Fun

My life has no purpose, no direction, no aim, no meaning, and yet I'm happy. I can't figure it out. What am I doing right?
—Charles Schulz

Am I having fun? Is my life exciting and happy? Well, no one really expects to live a completely joyful and ecstatic life all the time. But I do deserve to be happy and have fun most of the time. For many of us, fun gets pushed into the background of our lives, playing second fiddle to "important things" like work. It's easy to lose perspective. Men are socialized to be "achievement-oriented," although without a sense of fun in our work, we don't take much satisfaction in it. Just a pile of achievements, by themselves, don't give us a great feeling.

Right now get a pencil and a piece of paper. Write down five activities that are the most fun for you. Think about it! After you have made your "fun list," jot down the date of the last time you did that activity. Now look at your list. When was the last time you had fun, doing what you really love to do? If you have not done any of the things on your list in the past week, you are missing out!

Today I'm going to put aside time and do something just for fun. If I wait for the perfect time or the perfect place, I'll wait forever. The time to have fun is now.

211. An Invitation to Play

Suffer the little children to come unto me, and forbid them not; for of such is the kingdom of God.

—Mark 10:14

Some mornings I wake to the sound of small stones *pinging* against my bedroom window.

It's him again, that small tousle-haired boy I once was. These days he's appearing more and more frequently to befriend me. I raise my window and look into his clear eyes as he yells, "Can you come out and play today?" I want to yell back, "Yes!"

I don't play nearly enough. Sometimes I rationalize that "my work is my play." Today I won't kid myself. I'm going to walk through the gate that separates me from that timeless world where I could kick a can all the way down the street, just for fun. I will say "Yes!" to that little boy.

I will spend some part of today at play.

212. Living Toward Transformation

July 30

We are born Princes and the civilizing process makes us frogs.

—Eric Berne

The Chinese sages say we come into the world like an uncarved block. Throughout our lives, everyone we meet—parent, teacher, hero, or friend—has a part in shaping who we are.

Now as adults, we have the challenge of becoming more active in that shaping process. We keep what has served us, and throw out what hasn't worked. This is creative masculinity. To participate in this creative act requires courage, support, self-love, time, and most of all, patience. We are all princes, some better disguised than others. Throwing off our disguises, we strike out to find our rightful home: the kingdom within ourselves.

Today I will make some effort—big or small—to release the froggish, untrue parts of myself so that the majestic can be revealed.

213. Faith and Vice

Our faith comes in moments; our vice is habitual. Yet there is a depth in those brief moments which constrains us to ascribe more reality to them than to all other experiences.
—Ralph Waldo Emerson

One good way to live in the present and prepare for the future is to go back into the past for its teachings. The wisdom to be found in nineteenth-century American literature can feed the soul. Emerson and the other New England Transcendentalists discovered truths that still have meaning and validity today as we approach the twenty-first century. We can be so hard on ourselves when we falter. Emerson helps us to accept our humanity, if we would listen to his counsel.

"Vice" is an old-fashioned word; sometimes today we use the word "addiction" to cover the same terrain. Vices and addictions arise in part from our disconnection from the earth. We attempt to replace that primary and essential connection with substances and behaviors that rob us. Faith in oneself, in others, in our supporting ground, and in a Higher Power are essential for feeling whole and for resisting the desire to turn to substances such as alcohol and behaviors such as overeating that diminish us. Such faith comes in moments of heightened clarity and deeper vision.

Today I will name the vices that I recognize as mine, and seek the faith I need to leap into a new reality.

214. At Home in the Body

When Soul is present, nature is alive.
                    —Thomas Moore

We sometimes find ourselves surrounded by plants and trees, birds and animals, without really seeing them or taking in their beauty and their subtle teachings. It happens when our Soul is off-center. Ignoring where we are, we let our minds wander: dreaming of a new car, planning a trip, or fantasizing about someone attractive. In such a state our Soul seems to be missing, trapped somewhere far away from us, unable to move.

Time, recovery, and sharing the inner work with other men helps our Soul to find its rightful home. It may still go out for short walks, but it always finds its way back to the body where it belongs. When our Soul is centered in the body, we are one with our surroundings. We're available to receive what life offers.

Today I'll trust that when my Soul is at home in my body, I feel at home in the world. Then all I see looks back at me with blessings, and I experience a satisfaction that nothing outside me can bring.

215. Opening

Trust and its sister, surrender, are like a womb in which all of consciousness can gestate and mature.

—Richard Moss

We have closed down our bodies and our emotions to fend off so many pains: the pain of childhood and adolescence, the pain of conflict. We pulled a heavy darkness over ourselves, hoping to shield ourselves from events that might send us into grief and despair, even suicide. Many of us even closed our hearts to anyone who seemed to love us. We stayed leery of love.

Now, like the long-dormant blossoms of an ancient tree, we men are opening—some very rapidly, others more slowly. Many of us are open and ready for the new business of the world, having worked for years on unfinished business in recovery meetings, therapy, and men's groups. Whatever our timetable, our blossoming happens perfectly. Each of us contributes his own unique qualities to make this "tree of manhood" a thing of powerful beauty.

All we ask is time to adjust, to create a safe place for ourselves. We must ask our friends, lovers, and family to be patient with our opening process. We must also welcome the opening they must do themselves to join in courage with us.

Today I'm going to open up and show my heart just a little more. Remembering that it is useless to try to "force" myself to grow faster, I will give myself the rest and safety I need.

216. Being My Own Best Father

The fabled musk deer searches the world over for the source of the scent which comes from itself.

—Ramakrishna

Some of us men miss our dead fathers so much that rather than bury them emotionally and go on with our lives, we keep them alive in our heads. At certain times the father's voice speaks when the son's voice should be heard. Others of us, whose fathers are still alive, keep setting ourselves up, providing them opportunities to shame us. All the while we hope they'll be the dads they never were and can't be now. By continually setting our fathers—alive or dead—on the throne of our inner world, we keep ourselves from living fully.

Our time to be fathered by our fathers is gone, and we must grieve it. Today we're becoming good fathers to ourselves. We are becoming the men who, as children, we always wanted, needed, and longed to be with. By letting go of the fathers we had, we can start parenting ourselves. This carries a double blessing. Not only does it free us from seeking approval from Dad, it brings us into the present, where, as men, we come to a new understanding of our fathers. From there it's a short walk to lasting compassion, for them and for ourselves.

Today I'm going to talk to myself the way I wish my father had: "You're doing good work," "I'm proud of you," "Take your time. Keep trying, you'll get it."

217. Mentors

Tell me whom you admire and I will tell you what kind of a person you aspire to become.
—Sam Keen

If at some point in our lives we find a mentor, we are blessed. But a man who has not let his father go, who hasn't stopped acting the son to the men around him, risks misusing his mentor. By clinging to the "dream father," the father he never had, he projects his unmet needs on to this man. He may feel abandoned if his mentor doesn't spend as much time with him as he'd like, or doesn't return his phone calls as quickly as he thinks he should.

Men must not expect their mentors to be anything but flesh and blood. Mentors can't be our daddies or our saviors. The mentor we select may still be healing his own wounds, recovering at his own pace, just as we are. We may need the mentor's words, his art, his wisdom, and his knowledge, but we have no real *right* to them. If he withdraws from us, we can only grieve —never demand. But if he gives, we can feel privileged and honored.

Today I'll honor my mentor for his gifts to me. I'll stay open as well to guiding someone younger who can use a share of my experience, strength, and hope.

218. Fierceness

In every relationship something fierce is needed once in a while; both the man and the woman need to have it.

—Robert Bly

Fierceness can be life-enhancing. It comes with the wildness and determination of wild animals and is quite natural. Fierceness in the face of threats enables us to survive. Appropriate fierceness can protect tenderness. If we lose our fierceness we lose a certain passion, resolve, and spontaneity. Fierceness sets boundaries and protects. Timely fierceness can prevent disasters. Fierceness is a stance that enables a human or other life-form to maintain integrity in the face of forces that might damage.

Fierceness can also become distorted, overextended, and harmful. Fierceness is life-preserving and should not be seen as merely aggressiveness or meanness. When we express fierceness properly, we actually reduce our need to be aggressive. Fierceness helps get one up mountains and across lakes.

How much fierceness do I have? Too much, too little, or an appropriate amount? Am I fierce when I should be tender? Or tender when I should be fierce? Is there someone from whom I can learn appropriate fierceness? I may want to find a mentor or model for fierceness.

219. Spirit of Place

AUGUST 6

What makes a place special is how it buries itself inside the heart.

—Richard Nelson

Place is important—where you were born, where you have been, where you are right now, and where you will be. Explore the main places of your life—physically, emotionally, spiritually. Each of us is drawn to distinct places, depending partly on where else we have been, internally as well as externally. Do you prefer living on a coast, by a river or a lake, in the mountains, in a desert, or on a plain?

Do you have a secret place? Did you have one as a child? Someplace you once went, or go now, where your soul can manifest itself? You may want to remember such a place, or imagine one, and transport yourself there now.

Many men move around a lot in their lives. Each place has its own ways, its own spirit. Some of these ways seem to resonate more with us than others.

Today I will go where I am drawn—to see and perhaps to live. I will stay where I feel the energy is right for me.

220. Battling Fear

*Did I not tell you to look well, that those were
nothing but windmills?*
            —Miguel de Cervantes Saavedra

When we get tired or stressed, our mind
often creates giants with whom we feel we
must do battle. Many of us were raised
as prospective soldiers and were taught
that life is a win-or-die situation. When
we treat our mind as an adversary, our
negative thinking has already begun to
triumph over us. Then anxiety and sleep-
lessness take their toll.

Yet when we take time for a prayer, a
good meal, friendly support, and a good
night's sleep, we begin to see that most of
our "windmills" are made to spin by the
energy of fear.

*Today, before charging out against imaginary
enemies, I'll stop and tell a trusted friend
about my situation. I'll listen to a reasonably
objective view of my worries, rather than
struggle against myself.*

221. Spontaneity

When things are going by plan, the soul sleeps.
—Murray Stein

Sometimes we become addicted to our plans. If our plans don't work out, our day —even our lives!—may seem ruined. Relying heavily on plans can turn us into grim tourists passing through our lives according to a fixed and rigid schedule. Better if we could be curious sojourners, encountering each new mystery with enthusiasm and wonder.

Most men need structure, stability, and solidity. But we must also make room and time for our souls to awaken, to be open to the purely spontaneous occurrence, to revel in the unanticipated challenge, to enjoy the happy accident. Through flexibility we discover our creative insight.

Today I'll only plan what must *be planned, leaving some of my time unstructured and unrehearsed. Today I give myself the gift of spontaneity.*

222. Relocating the Search

The real voyage of discovery consists not in seeking new landscapes, but in having new eyes.

—Marcel Proust

The grass isn't greener on the other side of the valley. It's just different, full of mystery. And there is much uncharted territory right under our feet. We could go elsewhere if we like, but we're certain to find the same unfinished business we were facing, or avoiding, back at home. Still, sometimes we have to jump the fence that surrounds us. When we need to break free from an old perspective, roaming awhile can do a lot of good.

The most fruitful journey isn't an exterior kind of wandering. It's exploring our interior landscape. A silent walk, a weekend retreat, a time-out from relationship and responsibility allows us to discover new ground inside ourselves. On this journey we may need time to see things anew, to contemplate the challenges before us. We may need to grieve deeply to renew our search. This is not a blind quest, but a kind of roaming that clears the eye, empowering us to see the truth in our own interior.

Today, my vision fresh, I'll wander within. I'll see opportunity in every peak and valley. I'll rediscover how green and fertile my inner life can be.

223. Care

When you take care of something, it lives a long time.

—Zen master Dainin Katagiri

Care can be done in many ways, and there are many people and things warranting our care. Some ways of caring are vigorous and direct, others are more subtle and indirect. Some people are really good at caring by gift-giving, others by providing nurturing environments.

Masculinity is something that needs caring, like an orchid. It is too often taken for granted. When ignored, it is endangered. When cared for, it can thrive. Men are more fragile than we sometimes admit. Some of us men have difficulty surrendering ourselves to care. This can literally be dangerous—for example when we are sick and need the care of another, either a friend or a professional. When men care for each other, the results can be wonderful.

How do you want to be cared for? Go ahead and admit that at times you do want to be cared for. This does not mean that you are weak and dependent. It means you are more fully a man.

224. Walking

Perhaps the truth depends on a walk around a lake.

—Wallace Stevens

How about a good walk today? Men used to walk many hours each day. Thoreau walked three to four hours every day. Walking has many special pleasures—changes of sight, smell, and feelings. We can walk just for the sake of walking, not necessarily to get anywhere or to achieve a certain goal, just to walk—moving one foot before the other. Walking grounds us, reminding us that we were made to be earth-bound creatures.

Walking can transform our consciousness, thinking, and feeling. Ideas often come to us as we walk, so it can be wise to carry a small booklet. Walking uses many parts of the body, including the legs and the eyes, some of our biggest and some of our smallest parts, united in a common activity. The activity of walking is life-enhancing. There are many good reasons for walking: to be with oneself, to see the surroundings, to change one's consciousness, to expend energy, to get somewhere. Walking with someone is a good way to get to know him. You may even want to walk without your usual shoes—perhaps only in socks, or sandals, or even barefoot. Notice the sensations as your foot hits the ground. Try walking in different places—by a river, up a hill or mountain, by the shore of a lake or an ocean.

I will stretch out my legs today and go for a walk. What do I notice along the way? Outside myself? Inside myself? I allow my eyes to move in all directions—up, down, and about. I allow myself to feel whatever comes up.

225. Exploring Silence

Silence is deep as Eternity; speech is shallow as Time.

—Thomas Carlyle

When I get scared, afraid, and full of anxiety, I may feel compelled to fill the air with talk. I may be saying nothing of substance, but still, the noise is somehow comforting to me. It affirms that I'm here, that I'm active and alive. The sound of the spoken word can be a wonderful tool for healing, yet I must learn to feel the value of silence. I can do this by surrounding myself with quiet, instead of the sound of my voice.

Today, instead of talking the fear away, I will sit in the center of silence for a while. I'll practice silence by letting someone else speak, by listening intently to the silence between each word.

226. Returning the Earth

We have conquered the environment, and in our obsession for control, we no longer allow the environment to live in us.
—Valerie Andrews

Humankind has "tamed" the wilderness, bought and sold land for profit and loss. For too long we have mortgaged the earth and bankrupted its resources, pouring fumes into the skies and sludge into the oceans as if they were ours to destroy. Much more than rhetoric and legislation is needed to change this pattern of control and conquest over nature. I must begin a new inner relationship to my environment. Only then will the right action be clear to me.

I resolve to let the great trees live in me. I accept their strength and the wisdom of their years. I invite the land back into my legs and back and bones so that I might reclaim the rhythms of birth, death, and renewal. As I stand on the shore, I'll feel the sea rushing into my gut. I'll let my arms reach to embrace the painted sky. I'll walk right through the mud! I'll receive the meaning of those mountains at which I used to blankly stare, wondering who "owned" them. To be truly alive, I must relinquish my illusions. To truly survive, I must learn to receive the grace of this earth with gratitude, respect, and love.

Today I let go of the illusion of control, the dogma of dominion. I set my soul on automatic pilot, letting it soar through this world. Today I am touched and taught by the earth.

227. A Shield of Words

AUGUST 14

Words, as is well known, are great foes of reality.

—Joseph Campbell

Sometimes, particularly when I'm scared, I tend to talk too much. I hide behind a shield of words. I used to talk and talk to drive my fear away, but more often I ended up driving out someone I loved. The fear did disappear for a while, but I found it years later: in my lower back, in my butt, my shoulders, my jaw, and in my heart. Now I'm committed to feeling that fear but then letting it pass through me.

I still appreciate words, especially the way they shorten the distance between us. Words help me share my joys and disappointments, my tenderness and encouragement. Still, I can't always be sure that my meaning is coming through to others, even when we speak the same language. But ah! hugs, kisses, a gentle touch to the cheek, holding a child's face tenderly in the hands, and feeling the love that flows out through the eyes—these communicate what can never be said with words.

Today I will speak less and mean more.

228. Grief, or Self-Pity?

What soap is for the body, tears are for the soul.

—Jewish proverb

Most men have not witnessed grieving done in a healthy way. What we have seen is mostly self-pity, which is less a feeling than a repetitious pattern of thinking about the past. Self-pity does have a purpose, though: it alerts us that we probably need to grieve.

Here's what healthy grief looks like: My father dies, or my wife leaves, and I wake up every day and weep until my body doesn't want to weep anymore. I shower and shave, and even though I'm still dripping when another wave of grief or anger comes over me, I let the tears and anger wash through my body. I make myself a healthy breakfast and eat it, even though my appetite is poor. I write a letter that probably won't ever be sent, expressing all the unspoken words inside. I feel everything that aches to be felt, and all without a trace of shame or judgment. I don't listen to anyone who tells me, "It's not that bad," or "Things could be worse," because such statements are the sign of a closed heart. I stay near two or three trusted friends, or a group that can support me. I go to people who'll listen patiently while I tell my story until I don't need to tell it anymore.

Today I'll grieve the losses I need to grieve. When the feelings need to be released, I can naturally let them go.

229. Zaniness

Start a huge, foolish project,
like Noah.
It makes absolutely no difference
what people think of you.

—Rumi

One of the endearing qualities of men is our zaniness—our willingness to go off on some wild, foolish project. Travel projects, for example, can be great fun. Imagine yourself in some faraway place. Building projects can also be exciting. Imagine yourself building your perfect home. It is important to understand and act on our yearnings.

We have become overly rational in our time, having lost some of our boy wildness. Watching a group of boys, we notice how they often experiment and do zany things. Adult men have a lot to learn from boys. A life without zaniness and a circle of friends without zany ones is missing something. We are fortunate when we have zany men in our lives. We need to keep from becoming too serious.

Do you have any zany friends? Or can you think of characters in movies or books who are zany? What do you feel about them? Do they repulse you? Or are you drawn to them?

230. Divine Will

Explore daily the will of God.

—Carl G. Jung

Within me is a strong *will*: a will to know, to excel, to be recognized, to feel powerful. My self-will is filled with desire and longing to be noticed and to feel important. It is my will that pushes me to overcome others for my own gain, that encourages me to act in ways that violate my own highest standards. Left unchecked, my will attempts to fill my mind, my heart, and my life with possessions and meaningless toys. My will is not a bad thing; it can be put to excellent use as a strong ally on the spiritual path. But when left unchecked and unguided by a Higher Will, my small self-will seeks to manipulate people and events, due to its fear of the unknown.

If I seek the will of God *first,* I tap into a source of power, a clarity of vision, that is impossible to get from my own undirected will. Finding God's will for me is the ultimate prize, the most rewarding goal, the jewel in the crown of life. In searching for God's will, I lose nothing that was truly my own, nor do I need to give anything up. Instead, by steadily seeking the Will of a Higher Power, my life is flooded with tender amazement and innumerable blessings.

I can remind myself throughout the day to seek God's will by repeating silently, "Thy Will, not mine, be done."

231. Individuality

There never has been one like me before, and there never will be one like me again.
—Howard Cosell

Each of us is unique and precious. We have different talents, different dreams, and different fears. One man may love to dance and drum in the company of other men, while another loves the quiet solitude found in reading a book. Our differences should be nurtured and encouraged. What a dull life it would be if everyone were the same!

When we men gather in groups, our differences spark our creativity. Much has been written and said about the importance of being a "team player." There's a reason for this: there's power in a team. The most effective teams, however, recognize that their power lies in their "collectiveness," in the grouping of so many unique talents and skills.

Today I will honor my individuality by recognizing my own abilities and strengths.

232. Wake Up!

Do you have a body? Don't sit on the porch!
Go out and walk in the rain!
　　　　—Kabir (translated by Robert Bly)

Kabir's message applies to men today, though he wrote it in the fifteenth century in India. We are too often too asleep. Walking in the rain is one of the many things that can wake us up. Waking up is not something you do once and for all. It must be done over and over again. Waking up is a continuous process, as is going back to sleep. Being awake is risky. It takes courage. To be awake is to notice. To notice is to decide what to do. And there's the rub. So often we fall into passivity.

　　Many men today need a wake-up call. Much of masculinity has been stunned, shocked by forces such as industrialism. We have been taken from our natural habitats and often away from our bodies. Our work today tends to lack contact with the land and our hands. We have lost much of the intimacy that grows up in apprenticeships and villages. Yet there is much that can wake us up—a teacher, a lover, a work of art, a child, an animal, an aspect of nature.

Today I will practice being awake and alert. When I am fully present there is so much energy and so much to enjoy.

233. Intimacy and Distance

Once the realization is accepted that even between the closest people infinite distance exists, a marvelous living side-by-side can grow up for them, if they succeed in loving the expanse between them.
— Rainer Maria Rilke (translated by Stephen Mitchell)

Things that appear contrary are sometimes in fact linked—like night and day, men and women, the sun and the moon. Intimacy and distance are linked at the core. Appropriate distance-taking can preserve intimacy and relationships.

Geographical distance, like absence, can make the heart grow fonder. Some modern couples, especially mature ones, organize their homes to facilitate both contact and distance. Sometimes one member of the couple, often the man, needs more distance, and the other, often the woman, needs more closeness. Affirming the closeness while taking some distance can be essential. Statements such as, "I'm leaving now because I need some space," can help. Both distance and closeness can contribute to intimacy.

What amount of distance do I need, geographical or otherwise, to preserve intimacy? How can I make that distance?

234. Search for the Sword

Though much is taken, much abides;
* . . . that which we are, we are—*
One equal temper of heroic hearts,
Made weak by time and fate, but strong in
*   will*
To strive, to seek, to find, and not to yield.
                    —Alfred, Lord Tennyson

Most of us received no sword from our fathers. Instead we inherited an awkward club, or an attitude, or a wound. So we say "yes" when we mean "no." We pound our point into the ground, and we abuse others with our foul dispositions.

All the while we wish for a sword sharp enough to amputate our dysfunction, to cut through the crap daily life can dish out, to sever the umbilical cords that bind us to people and places in our history. We want a sword that gleams in the darkness, that lights our way, that shines for those less fortunate or those too small or weak to stop the abuse they're receiving. We must find this sword and remove the dust it has collected. Then we must learn when to wield it and when to sheath it.

Today I'll search for this sword. When I find it, I'll keep it close by: in my briefcase, my pocket, my soul.

235. Removing My Armor

Armor is fine, but it keeps you from knowing what the weather is like.

—William Stafford

For many of us, the climate in our childhood home was often cool or cold—the silent, frosty stares and emotional distance made us feel frozen inside, until after years we seemed not to care about ourselves or anyone else. At other times the heat of our parents' anger—whether vented on us physically or through fiery words—made us want to escape from our body altogether. It was during such moments that we first put on the armor we wore as we entered into relationships with others.

Now, many years later, our desire to feel the weather again has reemerged. We want to know the reality of being with our lovers, friends, family. We take off the armor one piece at a time, going slowly, gently, because we realize we're not just uncovering our joy; we're uncovering our wounds, too. It is a delicate undertaking, but well worth it. We welcome the wind and rain, the tears as well as the sunlight of smiles and tenderness. The love we've longed for pours into our life when we remove our helmets, our breastplates, our shields.

Today I'll remove my armor with care, allowing myself some safety as I challenge the old fears that imprisoned me.

236. Fire

The voice at the center speaks in tongues of flame. . . . The child in man hears his fire rise.

—M. C. Richards

The author of the quotation above, M. C. Richards, is a potter. Fire is at the center of her art, as it is at the center of much art—indeed, of life itself. The blaze captures our gaze. Love, like fire, can sear, is not always kind, can cut through the dead wood, demanding change. Solar fire lights each day; without it we would perish instantly. The sun rises brilliantly some mornings, giving us pleasure and another new day. The sources of fire are many: relationships, the sun, a forest burning wildly, and wherever friction exists. Fire is many things: strength, power, destruction, beauty.

Some people so fear fire that they never allow its flames to ignite them. They become passive, missing the activity inherent in fire. Others move too often into the fire and are frequently burned. Crafting the appropriate relationship to fire and to fiery people is key.

Today I will reflect on fire. I may light a fire in a fireplace, or make a fire on a beach, in my backyard, or elsewhere. As I watch the flames leap, I will think about how to kindle the fire in my heart.

237. Feeling My Life

The ultimate guide of conscious life is a sense of mystery that encompasses it.
—Lewis Mumford

It's so easy to shift into automatic pilot, to zip through the day without really being aware of living. Have you ever driven a car without even thinking about what you were doing, and then been surprised when you got to your destination because you didn't remember anything about the trip? We often live in the future, thinking intensely about something that might happen later, oblivious to what is happening at the moment.

Many of us live much of our lives on autopilot. When we stop and pay attention to life as it is happening, we really *feel* alive. We *experience* living. We have been socialized to plan and think, but to neglect our "feeling self." It is through our inner feeling, however, that we engage in life. To break out of this state, all we have to do is focus on what we are feeling. Throughout the day we can ask ourselves, "What am I feeling right now?" When we pause to experience our emotions, we are often surprised.

Today I'll take a feeling break. Stopping for a moment, I'll ask, "What am I feeling right now?" I will remain open to whatever I am experiencing.

238. Expressing Feelings

The action of the soul is oftener in that which is felt and left unsaid than in that which is said in any conversation.

—Ralph Waldo Emerson

When a feeling such as grief is blocked, it may find expression in another form, such as anger. It is important to try to match the inner feeling with the outer expression. Our society has not always accepted men who express the full range of masculine feelings, causing us to vent certain emotions—such as sorrow and sadness—in more "acceptable" ways, such as anger.

Feelings range widely. They are guides, signs to what is happening inside. Sometimes they come in opposites—such as excitement and fear. A feeling in the moment may remind us of a previous feeling. Our family of origin can deny us our feelings as children, rejecting them. Getting back to one's own feelings—beyond the judgments of family and friends—is important.

It can be difficult to express our feelings. At other times it is hard to contain them. Certain behaviors—crying, for example—reveal feelings. Journal writing is another outlet that can help a man realize his own feelings and track them over time. You decide; they are your feelings. Express or contain them as you desire.

How do you express your feelings? Are you satisfied with their expression, or might you expand your range?

239. Integrity

Learn to see . . . listen . . . and think for yourself.

—Malcolm X

Sometimes I get so caught up in trying to say what I think other people want to hear that I lose my own unique ideas. This form of "people pleasing" erodes my self-esteem and my integrity. By constantly trying to please others, I ultimately lose my ability to think for myself.

It's all right to agree with others, but not at the expense of my own values. Even though I may feel hesitant to "rock the boat" by expressing my own thoughts and beliefs, it is essential that I give voice to my own truth and my own values. This does not mean pounding my point into the ground. It simply means that I present my own perspective and respect it as worthy of consideration.

Today I will stand firm in my values. I will not be swayed into taking any action that my heart does not condone.

240. Friendship

True friendship comes when silence between two people is comfortable.
—Dave Tyson Gentry

Friendships add rich color to the tapestry of my life. My friends are companions and fellow travelers who support and love me without judgment and attachment. They are men and women who listen when I talk, and who allow me to be quiet when I need to be silent. These are the companions I choose to spend my time with. They are my family of choice.

I receive so much of value from my friends. Still, if I do all the giving or all the taking, all the talking, or all the listening, the friendship will really be one based on dependence; frustration and resentment will surely result. In the give-and-take of a healthy friendship, I take my turn listening and being supportive. If my friends and I want to be on equal footing, we must each support the other.

Today I will honor and acknowledge a friend through my giving as well as my taking.

241. Loving Freely

Be assured that if you knew all, you would pardon all.

—Thomas à Kempis

Every time we try to change another person's behavior, we are moving in the direction of the past, ultimately toward a parent we wanted to change and couldn't. Spending time and energy to struggle against another's way of being is demeaning to that person and belittling to ourselves. Much as we'd like to tell ourselves otherwise, such a struggle does not arise from love, and it wears us out.

We can't change another person. We know the truth of this when we remember how hard and how often we've tried. We might just as well stand on the shore, commanding the tide to turn, or attempt to stop the seasons from changing.

A new approach is possible: we can look on those around us as perfect expressions of themselves, and appreciate the differences between us. We don't have to agree or surrender our own values in order to love freely. We only have to surrender our desire to control events. If we do, then we're free to reap the benefits of this more peaceful way of life.

Today I don't want to "convert" my loved ones to my perspective. I'll practice minding my own business and shift my attention to changing the only person I can change—myself.

242. Deep Respect

Our capacity for intimacy is built on deep respect, a presence that allows what is true to express itself, to be discovered.

—Jack Kornfield

Respect can connect humans at the deepest level. Love that is based on respect—rather than need or longing—is more enduring. Such respect can tolerate great differences. Truth and commitment can emerge in the container of mutual respect.

Some things command our respect—perhaps because of their beauty or power. Respect for the ordinary, especially in intimate relationships, can sustain those connections. Express your respect. Say it. Show it in a gift or gesture, especially during difficult times. That which is accompanied with respect, even if it is difficult, will be better heard.

Today I will respect myself and all others whom I have contact with. I will communicate that respect by what I do and say.

243. Acceptance

We will not regret the past nor wish to shut the door on it.
    —The Big Book of Alcoholics Anonymous

There are times when our past seems to reach out and grab us. In those moments the past becomes a living presence, controlling our thoughts, emotions, and behavior. When this happens we become stuck, even fearful, and it may seem we can feel nothing but regret and guilt.

But when we can embrace our past without a struggle, it loses its power and we become free of it. Accepting ourselves is the key to freedom from our past. We are still responsible for our past behavior, but we can forgive ourselves for our mistakes and move on. We can learn from the past; we do not have to live in it.

Today I will accept all of my past, the triumphs and the mistakes.

244. Fathering

It is a wise father that knows his own child.
—William Shakespeare

For many of us, as we were growing up, our fathers were mostly absent from our lives. They were away at work, or drinking, or sitting silently in front of the TV. They could not give us the emotional connection that we inwardly yearned for. Even when they were physically present, they weren't really available.

Now that many of us are fathers ourselves, we sometimes wonder what we can give to our children. We had no strong male role models to show us how to nurture and love children actively. We are finding that, even though fatherhood is uncharted territory for us, we can be loving and nurturing fathers. As we heal from the wounds of our past, we let go of the addictions and the rage. In this healing we find the part of us that can nurture and love a child.

Today I will share myself with a child.

245. Work

He who will do his own work well, discovers that his first lesson is to know himself, and what is his duty.
— Michel Eyquem de Montaigne

The truth is that great things happen through me. There is beauty in what I do, whether I am listening to children, writing a poem or a letter, fixing dinner, repaying a debt, or being there for a friend. I must remember to look at what I have made, the ways I have served, and the changes I am striving to make in my own character. All of these are valuable and elegant.

Today I will take time to appreciate myself for the work I do in this world.

246. Play

The mass of men lead lives of quiet desperation. What is called resignation is confirmed desperation. . . . There is no play in them, for this comes after work.
—Henry David Thoreau

Children play. It is their nature. How little support we get, as men, to play. By not playing we neglect much of what it means to be alive. Or our play as adults is compulsive, aggressive, competitive, driven—not at all like the natural play of children, which is devoted to exploring, to learning, to trying out new identities and ways of being.

Men are too often work objects, punching in nine to five. Most of the work needed to fuel industrial and postindustrial societies requires us to numb our feelings. A dullness persists after work, leaving us no energy or spirit to play. In failing to play we neglect much of what it means to be alive.

Bringing spontaneous play into the adult lives of men is a key remedy to what Thoreau describes as resignation and confirmed desperation. We would benefit from returning to some of the play of boys on drums and in sandboxes. Play is literally life-enhancing. Men playing together is a wonderful sight.

Today I will imagine myself playing in some way and enjoying it. I will find things I enjoy doing, like participatory sports, that put me in contact with this spirit of play. I may invent new things to do. I may observe children playing, relearning from them.

247. Sacred Space

Sacred space is a place where human beings find a manifestation of divine power, where they experience a sense of connectedness to the universe. There, in some special way, spirit is present to them.

—J. Donald Hughes

There are places of power in the world where we can feel the very universe resonate with our soul. In these sacred places we draw strength and vision from the spiritual source that flows in and around all things. For some of us sacred space is found in churches, temples, and holy sites. Sacred space also occurs in nature, where forces create a special feeling of power and majesty.

We can also create our own sacred space—a place to go for spiritual renewal, to feel the power of the spirit, to pray and meditate. Find a place where you will be undisturbed. Bring to this place some of the things that are holy and spiritual for you—a book, perhaps, or an icon. Maybe you are drawn to natural artifacts: gems, feathers, wood. Follow your heart in selecting your sacred symbols. Then spend time in your sacred space.

You may wish to share this place with others, but select only those who support and understand your need for sacred space. Use this special place of power as a source of renewal and connection to the spirit. The more time spent there in reflection and contemplation, the more powerful this place will become for you.

Today I will visit my sacred space, or commit myself to creating one.

248. Honoring the Body

The body is ready to sing all night, and be entered by whatever wishes to enter the human body singing.

—Robert Bly

When we were small boys, our bodies recorded everything that came to them—the bright sunlight, the sound of criticism and the feel of a slap, the sensation of shame, the welcoming fur of a pet. Too often the hurts seemed to far outweigh the comforts, until hope, joy, and serenity felt far outside us.

These days, though, we're reclaiming that boy's body. It may appear a little wrinkled in places, but the boy is still inside it. We take this body with us like an old friend, giving him a hand out of the scrap heap, taking him to recovery meetings, men's groups, and gatherings where we can heal. Together we grieve and let loose our anger about all that has hurt us and all that we have lost. In the process, we're growing new arms to hold on with, new legs to stand firm, and a new heart open to love.

Today I'll release the pain I've held for so long in my shoulders, my back, my butt, and my bones. I'll fill my body instead with everything that sings to me.

249. Yawning

Yawning is an orgasm for your face. It's a letting go that ripples through your entire body.

—Gunver Ingeborg

We are in good company when we yawn. Ostriches, reptiles, dogs, cats, rats, monkeys, and even fish do it. We all open our mouths and let in air, thus changing our face—and more.

It is a fiction that we yawn because we are bored or sleepy. Yawning balances our body systems by bringing in oxygen and increasing circulation. Yawning releases the jaw and neck and can travel to the ears. Yawning relaxes the pelvis. It also relaxes the eye muscles, stimulating the production of tears to clear tired or dry eyes. A yawn encourages us to breathe deeply—to take in air and release tension and anxiety. Like crying or laughing, yawning is a form of discharge, catharsis, emptying. Some therapists have developed yawn counseling as a technique to encourage anxious clients to relax.

One person yawning in a group often causes others to do the same. Repressing a yawn produces tension in the jaw and elsewhere. If we contain our impulse to yawn, we shut down the natural functioning of the body.

Today I will give myself a big yawn—more than one—and stay with it for a while. I will experience the power yawning can have to transform the way I feel in my body.

250. Loving the Questions

SEPTEMBER 6

The greatest and most important questions of life . . . can never be solved but only outgrown.

—Carl G. Jung

All too often I've tried to be "Mr. Fix-it" or "The Answer Man." I sometimes succumb to the myth that, as a man, I should possess the skills and knowledge to make any problem disappear! I may indeed have great skills and fine knowledge, but is it always best to display these gifts? Sometimes the most generous response is simply to listen and be still.

When my loved ones come to me in bewilderment or frustration, I will not leap into action to fix their problems. Each of us is already whole. Allowing others their dignity, I affirm my own wholeness as well.

Today I'll be patient with myself and others when we are confused and questioning. I resolve to love the questions themselves, so that my clear inner knowledge can rise to the surface.

251. Initiation

One of the characteristics of the modern world is the disappearance of any meaningful rites of initiation.

—Mircea Eliade

Initiation introduces the candidate into the human community and into the spiritual world. Most societies throughout time have initiated their boys into manhood during their adolescent years. Initiations have been a traditional way of altering the consciousness of the boy and teaching him the community's values. The community of men initiated each boy, taking him from his mother. The youth had to face obstacles—perhaps a wild animal—and deal with his fears.

When men no longer offer this teaching to teenagers, the teenagers can become isolated or turn to each other in gangs. Today we have many such uninitiated men, who turn to addictions or violence—or both.

We need to rediscover rites of passage into manhood. We need to establish communities of men willing to cooperate in bringing boys into manhood. We uninitiated men may stumble as we seek ways to initiate each other and the younger ones now growing up. But let's dare to be awkward.

Today I will imagine how my life might be different had I been truly initiated into the community of men. I may choose to seek an opportunity to build connections to younger men by blessing them with initiation.

252. Eternal Value

The only ones among you who will be really happy are those who have sought and found how to serve.

—Albert Schweitzer

Jobs, creative work, producing—sometimes these become too big and too important, obscuring everything else in our lives. We so desperately hope our soul will be healed through accomplishments and achievements, that we lose sight of what is really valuable, real, and eternal.

Yet our work can wound us as much as it heals: we lose our jobs, our art doesn't become famous. At these times life comes into focus, when that which has real worth and value rises to the surface like the sun peeking over the lake. That which is most important is to be found in relationships: to our family, our friends, our health, our planet, our principles, our Higher Power. We need to be reminded of this fact from time to time, and life's challenges are the perfect reminders.

If we have things in perspective—if our conduct in relationships is at the top of our priority list—we will walk with wings. Everything will seem light and possible.

Today I remember that the value in my life is to be found in my relationships to others.

253. Showing Up

Eighty percent of success is showing up.
                              —Woody Allen

What would I be like now if my father had been present at all of my ball games, graduations, recitals? What if my father had been there when I wished for him, to say and do the kind things, the fair things? Maybe I'd be walking like a prince, expecting the best, showing up for my own life with more confidence, more love. Maybe. In any case, I can choose to show up today for my own life. In doing so, I'm making something better for myself, giving myself more than my father knew how to give.

I'm learning to show up, to be present in relationships, at men's meetings, at gatherings, and in my own recovery.

Today for a few moments I'll be present right in my own body, experiencing my life as fully as I can. I'll be present for a child, a lover, a friend, or just for myself.

254. Staying

The faith, rather, is that by staying, and only by staying, we will learn something of the truth . . . and it is always both different and larger than we thought.

—Wendell Berry

Many men know a lot about leaving, escaping, taking off for the sake of "getting the job done." We know less about staying, sitting still, and waiting patiently while the job gets done without so much effort. It's hard to believe sometimes that the work will get done without frantic action, but it's true.

"Stay" and "still" are beautiful words. Many a man wanted his father to stay, but he left, teaching one last lesson— how to fly—as he stood poised in the doorway, one foot in, one out. To be sure, there are times when we should go, but our leaving should be born out of love, not out of fear. Maybe we're afraid that our wives or lovers don't love us. We can't leave just because we're afraid. Of course, we can't stay out of neediness, or a sense of "obligation" either. Our duty is to understand ourselves, to feel our fear, and to know that commitment hurts sometimes. Maybe the thought of staying doesn't appeal to us. Maybe it doesn't seem "manly." Yet staying may be just the fire in which we can forge our masculinity. How are strength and courage to be tested, if not by facing fear when we'd rather run?

Today I'll take a searching look at the situations and the people I may have been leaving out of fear. Today I'll stay with them awhile, even if it's uncomfortable. My commitment to understanding, to truth, is worth it.

255. Holding

*Something we were withholding made us
    weak
Until we found it was ourselves.*

—Robert Frost

It is difficult to conceive of anyone who had been tenderly loved and caressed in infancy not learning to approach a woman or a child with especial tenderness.

—Ashley Montagu

Most men never learned to be held—held up, perhaps, when drunk or sick, but not *held* in the way women seem so easily to relax in the arms of another. So as boys we grew up learning to protect and defend, providing a shoulder for women and children to rest their heads on while they slept and we stayed on guard. So many men long for that kind of trust, comfort, and safety. Gradually through time, grieving, recovery, and support from strong men and women, we're learning to trust. We're learning to hold and be held.

Today I'll let myself want to be held. And then I'll trust someone enough to hold me for a while—not just give me a hug, but really hold me.

256. Thinking Less

I never came upon any of my discoveries through the process of rational thinking.
　　　　　　　　　　　—Albert Einstein

Men, especially, think too much. We are too often work objects with too much centering around our work and the thinking it requires. Thinking consumes so much of our time that we have less energy for other activities, such as feeling, daydreaming, and sailing—life-enhancing activities that some would consider useless, since they do not produce anything. Thinking can also be enjoyable, especially when it is not excessive, when it is done for pleasure and is not goal-oriented.

　　Some activities, such as drumming, can be hindered greatly by thinking. The hands know what to do, but the mind can get in the way, especially for those who have been overtrained to conceptualize, theorize, and analyze. There are times to let the mind go and the body, heart, or soul take over and direct our being.

Today, accepting that thinking sometimes gets in my way, I will quieten my mind through meditating or drumming or dancing.

257. Breath

Time is breath.

—G. I. Gurdjieff

Become aware of the breath. Take one minute, right now, to focus on breathing. . . . Breathing is our link to life and to the universe; it connects us to all the cycles of nature. Each inhalation is a taking-in, a receiving of the gift of Life. Each exhalation is a letting go, a giving back, a surrender. The natural expansion and contraction of breath keeps us in balance. When we stop breathing, or breathe in a constricted way, fear takes hold and we lose our balance.

Each time we take in the breath and let it go, a cycle is completed. Right now, for one minute, watch the breath flowing gently in and out. Count each cycle, without hurrying. . . .

How many times did the breath come in and go out in that one minute? What did it feel like to focus on counting breaths? Did this minute go quickly or did it seem slow; was time suspended? There is great value in being conscious of the breath. It makes us aware that we are alive in this moment.

Throughout this day I will take time to focus on the breath; each minute I spend in this way increases my awareness and vitality.

258. Women

What do we live for, if it is not to make life less difficult for each other?
—George Eliot (Mary Ann Evans)

So much has been said about relationships between men and women! Some have suggested that women speak a different language than I do, and that true understanding between the sexes is almost impossible. When I listen to so many voices predicting gloom and doom, my own hopeful inner voice sometimes gets lost among them.

Men and women are natural equals. We share a world. We share the responsibility for children, and for the well-being of all who live on this planet. Women don't have to earn my respect any more than I have to earn theirs. But our qualities are not the same. If I practice respecting the light in everyone I meet, I will naturally treat both men and women with dignity. Then understanding between us will arise of its own accord.

Today I will honor the women in my life by accepting them just as they are right now.

259. Returning Home

We will never find a way home until we find a way to look the caribou, the salmon, the lynx, and the white-throated sparrow in the face, without guile, with no plan of betrayal.
—Barry Lopez

The Earth is our home—and all its creatures our neighbors. We are here together, connected. Our home is beautiful, diverse, and full of possibility. Yet we often feel homeless, out of contact—with ourselves, with each other, and with the Earth itself. Our feelings of homelessness, even when we have a house, can lead us to addictive substances and behavior, as substitutes for the real thing.

Many of us live in cities. Urban dwelling has the advantages of employment opportunities and chances to be around other people. However, in the cities, humans have less contact with plants, animals, and wildness itself. Many of us live by a coast, a river, or a lake. Others live in forests. Some prefer deserts. The Earth is surely our home, and not just in its feminine form. The Earth is deeply masculine —erect mountains, exploding volcanoes, phallic flowers. Men have become distant and separate from the Earth. It is time to return.

What are the qualities of the Earth that I most appreciate? How does it support me and provide for me?

260. The Desert

In the desert we wait, we weep, we learn to live.

—Alan Jones

The desert—that sandy place away from the city and civilization—can be refreshing in its sparseness. Deserts in the Southwest possess great beauty; we can be richly rewarded by journeys there. The desert has the power to open vision and change what —and how—we see.

In the desert unexpected things move toward a man, often from inside. Deserts are for introspection, revelation, conversion, tribulation, and transformation. The desert is the mystic's home. Many spiritual leaders, such as Jesus, have spent important time in the desert, from which they experienced a clearing in their path.

In the desert it is easier to see what is essential—the ground below and the sky above. There is less clutter to distract. The important things, such as water, are clear. The desert can facilitate what Alan Jones in *Soul Making* calls "receptivity, contemplation, clarity, and moral courage." By doing strange things to how we see, the desert plays tricks with the imagination; it intensifies and magnifies experience. Heat, dust, and loneliness can make us appreciate the need for simple things such as food, shelter, and companionship.

The desert is one of those gifts that many of us do not see. We may carry the attitude that the desert is a harsh, stern place. It is that. But there is meaning in the desert's austerity. We can benefit from the desert's unusual gifts.

Today I will spend some time in the desert, in my mind or in the outer world.

261. The Forest

The forest is a process of interrelatedness. . . .
We must have forest areas that are never
touched. . . . We must never extinguish that
heritage.

—Merv Wilkinson

In forests one can feel the interconnected-
ness of everything—humans, animals,
plants, wind, ocean, all that is. Each forest
has its own unique blend of trees, soil, air,
bugs, plants, and animals. We can literally
smell the differences in forests. They each
look different in size, shape, and color.
Some forests have trees that soar high; others grow closer to the ground. Some are so
dry that they seem to invite fires. Others
are wet, as if they were brothers to the
ocean—rain forests. Some forests are so
tightly packed that they block out the sun,
as the giant redwoods in northern California do. Others are spacious, allowing for
ample sun. Forests are as individual and
as alive as groups of humans.

Forests cover, going up into the sky
and down into the soil, connecting these
two distinct worlds. Forests breed life and
they digest. It can be great fun to spend a
night in a forest and even sleep on its
floor. Our ancestors used to sleep in forests regularly; the forest provides a soft
bed of leaves on which to relax and rest
deeply. When we lose forests we lose contact with life.

Allow a forest to unfold before you in your
imagination. Go into that forest, perhaps an
ancient one, and walk through it—feeling and
listening. There is much to see, much to hear,
and much to feel.

262. The Near

*My hope is to acclaim the rewards of . . .
becoming fully involved with the near-at-hand,
of nurturing a deeper and more committed
relationship with home.*

—Richard Nelson

What is near you, right now? Look
around. Any surprises? Is this a familiar
place? Do you come here often? What can
you see for the first time? Where are you
reading this book? In a bedroom, sitting
room, library, study? Or do you read outside? Look around now. Lift your eyes
from the page and notice what they see
nearest you.

Too often, in our desire to seek the
new and the exotic, we miss what is closest. But we do not have to travel far to see
much. Knowing the near is important.
Outside and nearby one's own home there
is much mystery. Any nearby thing can be
seen afresh by looking at it from different
angles. If you do not like what you see
right now, rearrange it, either in your
mind or in actuality. Or move to be near
something else.

*What do I want to be near to today? How can I
better see that to which I am near? Today I will
nurture a deeper relationship to that which is
near.*

263. Where Is the Treasure?

If there is to be any peace it will come through being, not having.

—Henry Miller

As boys, many of us learned that having a lot of toys brought popularity. As teenagers, whoever had the first car was the center of attention. If we had more clothes, money, and athletic ability, we had more dates and others envied us. To this day, many of us still seek happiness in *things*— a better car, a gold credit card, a more spacious house—more, always more. Where is our satisfaction? Aren't the things we have now the things we wanted a few years ago and worked so hard to achieve? Where is the contentment, the enjoyment we expected to feel?

There's nothing wrong with possessions, of course. It's great to feel gratitude for what we've received in our lives. But if we feel driven to get more, to accomplish more and more, maybe our desire is misplaced. What we really want most is not to be found outside us. Throughout the ages, the wise ones have said that the love we give and receive in this life is all we take with us when it's over. Together we can focus on acquiring inner peace. Then by our example, we will leave our sons and daughters this great treasure, a wealth they can never lose.

Today I'll look at how much time I spend getting, how much I spend giving, and how much I spend just being. I have the power to change the focus of my time and life to reflect the highest good.

264. Focusing

Life is not a dress rehearsal for something that's going to happen later. It's happening right now. Pay attention.
—Anonymous speaker at a Twelve Step
conference

It's easy for the mind to slip off into fantasyland, daydreaming and planning for every possible contingency that may occur in life. We may spend hours in this trancelike state, off somewhere in the future or the past, ignoring life in the present. When we indulge this habit, we miss the great stuff that's happening in life right now. And there are blessings all over the place! To refocus on experiencing the present moment, we can ask ourselves three questions:

What am I doing right now?
What am I thinking right now?
What am I feeling right now?

These simple questions help us to position ourselves in the present. They help us stay aware of our life as an amazing flow of events that always begins *right now*. When we are aware of the present moment, we're truly alive, and we feel a natural joy.

To stay aware throughout this day, I will ask these three questions to position myself in the present.

265. Celebrating the Seasons of Our Lives

What is life? It is the flash of a firefly in the night. It is the breath of a buffalo in the wintertime. It is the little shadow that runs across the grass and loses itself in the sunset.
—Crowfoot

Sometimes in the hottest part of the day in the middle of a dry, seemingly eternal summer, there's a moment when a cool, clear vision of autumn is present. Right smack-dab in the midst of the saddest moments is a pinhole of joy. And in the joy, at its very center, is another sadness.

At the center of each season of a man's life, the next season is buried, waiting to emerge. If I look closely into a new baby's wrinkled face, I can see the wisdom of elderly eyes. And in the aged face of a ninety-year-old man, I can catch the bright glimmer of innocence.

How can I stay aware of the divinity of each moment? How does a man pass consciously through time?

Today I'll recognize the life stage I'm living now. I want to accept it, honor it, and celebrate it fully. Each season is an occasion for wonder, for sadness, for a song. Let me not miss a moment of this journey.

266. Attention

My experience is what I agree to attend to.
　　　　　　　　　　—William James

Each of us has his own focus of attention
—things that we are aware of, see, and
hear—among the many stimuli in the
world. Two people in the same situation
notice quite different things. Being aware
of our attention can help us understand it
and modify it when we want. It can bring
us into present time, with our full range of
powers as human beings. Our awareness
can help us concentrate when we want to.
An art form or a glimpse of nature's
beauty can often change our attention,
bring in new images, and transform our
interior sight.

　　We attend to things in the inner and
outer worlds simultaneously. What do
you notice right now in your outer world?
What do you see? What grabs your attention? Where do you linger? Awaken all
your senses and notice the information
they report. Now what do you notice in
your inner world? What is your inner dia-
logue like today? Is it serene or chaotic? Is
it familiar or something new for you?

*Today I will take note of what my attention
focuses on. I will notice what I see and hear. I
will notice what is important to me. If I choose
to, I will also refocus my attention, perhaps by
taking a walk.*

267. Dreams

The dream is the small hidden door in the deepest and most intimate sanctum of the soul.
—Carl G. Jung

In some tribal cultures, villagers get together in the morning and tell their dreams, seeking their guidance. This simple but elegant ritual binds the tribespeople in a sharing of deepest intimacy.

Dreams send us messages, if only we would listen and figure out how to decode them. Sometimes it helps to write the dream down. Or better yet to tell a friend our dreams, not so much to hear his interpretation as to hear the dream spoken out loud. So much goes on inside us. Even when we do not remember our dreams, their work continues, making us whole, balancing, integrating. Dreams reveal what we are carrying around inside our unconsciousness.

Dreams connect us to another world, revealing there is always more of that world than the part of which we are consciously aware.

Today I will open myself to remember my dreams of the night before, or of the night before that. I will tell a dream that I remember to a friend or a loved one.

268. Leaving the Myths, Living in the Moment

SEPTEMBER 24

We become obsessed with buying in, not being in.

—Valerie Andrews

Many of us swallowed whole the myths of manhood. We bought into the shallow fable that said a house, two cars, and a mortgage would provide the picture-perfect version of a happy, worthwhile existence. The myths told us that working overtime and bearing the pressure of buying on credit was worth it, even if it stole all our time from family, from ourselves. We were sold a bill of goods that threatened our health and our relationships.

Now we are learning to believe in the moment. Throwing off the old myths, we come into harmony with ourselves and others. Now is the time for us to get involved in the lives of children. Now is the time to listen to our partners' struggles. This moment holds infinite possibilities for growth. In it, we can be silenced by the beauty of true masculinity and ignited by the pure power of rest, rejoicing, and rejuvenation!

Today I choose to believe in myself, and in the values that emanate naturally from my truth. I shake off the myths, the untruths, both for my sake and the sake of those I love.

269. Memories

In endowing us with memory, nature has revealed to us a truth utterly unimaginable to the unreflective creation, the truth of immortality.

—George Santayana

There is an electricity in the air on a crisp September night. The edge of coolness, the changing afternoon light brings back the unmistakable sounds of fall: voices of schoolchildren, football games, the crackling of leaves underfoot.

I can be transported back in time. At times, for the sake of recovery, I've gone reluctantly back to revisit the painful scenes. But I can also journey back to the good moments—the good friends who made life bearable at unbearable times; first loves who helped take away the chill of adolescence like a wool blanket on a cool Friday night. These good moments do exist in my life, and in my memory.

Today I will take time to revisit good memories and appreciate them. Today I remember the first kiss of autumn.

270. Dealing with Anger

It is easy to fly into a passion—anybody can do that—but to be angry with the right person to the right extent and at the right time and with the right object and in the right way—that is not easy, and it is not everyone who can do it.
—Aristotle

My emotions are neither good nor bad. They are currents that pass through me, sometimes for a few minutes, sometimes longer—the weather fronts of my inner world. When I feel the emotion of anger, I experience a powerful force. Sometimes this energy may be so overwhelming that I explode with fury and rage. Or my anger may turn inward, where it can transform into resentment or depression. Yet the energy of my anger can be constructive, too. I can channel this powerful emotion to end an injustice or defend my integrity.

To deny my anger cripples me from within. To honor anger means to express it healthily, without hurting myself or others. When I express my anger honorably, I honor myself.

Today I can choose how I will respond to my anger.

271. Legacy

Who touches a father touches the son.
          —Ethiopian (Amharic) proverb

My father passed on to me what he had learned, both the good and the bad. He gave me his pain and his hopes, just as he inherited his own father's pain and hopes. This lineage of men, passing their sorrows, joy, and wisdom down through the generations, is as old as the human species.

What I received from my father, I took, but I also changed it. I didn't want to pass my pain on to my children. So I've changed and healed.

Today I will be conscious of what I am passing on to the children, the next generation.

272. Transforming Blame

I never blame myself when I'm not hitting. I just blame the bat and if it keeps up I change bats.

—Yogi Berra

So many men tend to blame themselves for every difficulty—a bad work situation, a dysfunctional relationship—as if they were the only ones having trouble in it, unable to communicate. The Buddha once said, "No blame, just grief." Blame changes nothing. Grief does. When we go back through our history, we discover how we learned so many unfulfilling behaviors. Blame will not heal the wound. Grief will. So will taking responsibility for ourselves. We want to discover and put to use whatever will enrich our lives. We don't want to keep on internalizing and duplicating the destructive behavior we learned as children. We know it is up to us. Blame is beside the point.

Today I'll identify what needs grieving and grieve it.

273. Side-by-Side Intimacy

He is my side-by.
—Elena Avila, R.N., New Mexican
curandero (folk healer)

Intimacy comes in many forms. Language is a common means of connecting with others that produces face-to-face intimacy, as does a romantic candlelit meal and lovemaking. However, much of male intimacy is established side-by-side, without much language: walking together, gardening, painting the house, playing sports, working on a long-term project. An early morning ride with male friends to a day of work can allow us to be together, connected, without a lot of language exchange. In some Native American cultures such friends are called "side-bys."

Men value this silent side-by-side intimacy. It is what happens, for example, when a group of men drum together. Few words pass, but there is much communication. The presence of another man at our side, especially a friend, can totally change a situation. It can break isolation and offer support. Such intimacy has value in itself; it can also help men to get important things done. When we have a difficult task to complete, it is helpful to have someone at our side.

Today I will think about the people I like to have at my side. I may not even know why it is that I like them; it need not be rational.

274. Love

I wished I'd a knowed more people. I would of loved 'em all. If I'd a knowed more, I would a loved more.

—Toni Morrison

I am not defined by my accomplishments or by the things I acquire; these will not live after me. What will have a lasting effect is the love I freely give. When I accept other people the way they are, I express my love. When, without expectation, I give freely of my time to help others, I express love. When I seek the peaceful center of my inner being, I express love—for myself.

Love is dynamic and flowing. To experience love I must let it flow out of me and touch others. Love unexpressed and contained diminishes me. The more I love without expectation of return, the more love is returned to me. I can never run out of love; there is an endless supply.

As I go out into the world today, I resolve to let my love for others show.

275. Accepting Reality

OCTOBER 1

A hundred worries affect their minds, myriad affairs weary their bodies. Expending their vitality, exhausting their spirit, they take the false to be real.

—Liu I-ming

Men worry a lot about things we can't control: lack of economic security, a child's illness, a partner who may someday decide to leave. The "what ifs" of life can consume us; hidden, our fear grows, until we're too frozen even to share our fear with someone else.

The inability to speak about such fears saps our strength and vitality. There are always people around who will tell us that our worries are all for nothing, that our fears are just illusions. But that doesn't calm the scared boy inside. We were told ages ago that we were weak because we wanted someone to come into the dark room with us, to look under the bed to make sure the goblins weren't real. And even now we're often told, "Just stop worrying." "Don't be silly." "Go back to sleep."

The trolls and goblins seemed real then and sometimes still do now. But these days we can turn with gratitude to those who can listen to our fears without shaming us, to people we can trust to look into the dark with us to help us face the monsters lurking there.

Today I'll find someone to tell about the worries that won't go away. If I share them, they won't have a chance to turn into trolls who gobble up my energy and serenity.

OCTOBER 2

Sex may bring pleasure or joy, but not identity. In fact, we are able to lose ourselves in loving sexuality only to the degree that we have found the self elsewhere.

—Sam Keen

Sometimes I don't feel like making love. I may just want to be held or touched nonsexually. Sometimes I'm scared or just distracted. Other times I've felt I needed to do something for my partner to "earn" the passion I was enjoying so much. Then my own needs would get lost in the process. I'd feel guilty when my lover didn't have an orgasm, or didn't have one as great as what I experienced. All this made for some very serious and heavy sexual encounters. Where was the fun?

As I move on in recovery, gathering support from other men, I'm taking less responsibility for my lover's sexual satisfaction. I'm beginning to drop the myth of the Perfect Lover, to give more room for my partner to ask for what she really wants, instead of wearing myself out trying to guess. It feels like I'm moving toward a whole new approach to my sexuality, one that's more natural to me, one that has more to do with love and less with performance.

Today I'll take full responsibility for saying what I want sexually. I can enjoy and listen to my body for direction and guidance about when to make love and when to just cuddle, whether to risk, and how, and with whom. I'll remember that sex is about expression, not oppression. I'll remember that it's play.

277. Howling

The wolf's howl is a rich, captivating sound, a seductive echo that can moan on eerily and raise the hair on your head.

—Barry Lopez

Wolves howl to assemble their pack, especially before and after a hunt; to sound an alarm, especially at the den site; to locate each other in a crisis; and to communicate across long distances. Wolves sometimes howl out of restlessness and anxiety. When wolves howl in groups they tend to wag their tails and frisk about, perhaps joyous for breaking loneliness. A wolf's howl is so powerful that it may carry six or more miles.

Animal behavior, as well as children's behavior, can be instructive to men. Howling can be great fun. It can be done alone or with a group of men. Dogs may join in. We can howl at the moon or with no concrete object in mind. Howling can open a special place in the male body. Howling can bring a group of men together. Making animal sounds can help men relate to other creatures. Bringing animal sounds into our voice can expand it. The sound is very ancient and primordial; it can resonate deeply.

When was the last time you howled? If you have not done it recently (because you probably did as a boy), go out and howl. If you need the cover of night, then wait until this evening. If you need a private place, then find one.

278. Quietness and Listening

Silence, more musical than any song.
— Christian Roselli

Beneath the too loud and distracting sounds, there are other things to hear. In addition to things that shout at us each day, there are things that whisper. They can be heard only in silence. Listen to them. Hear what may take straining to hear. You can literally train yourself to hear things that most people miss because they are focused on the loud, that which demands attention. Other voices, sounds, and messages exist beneath the roar that is usually there.

Give your attention today to the quiet, to what you may have missed before. Hear its music. Beneath the over-stimulating barrage of contemporary life there is an original silence that holds all of us. Wanting to feel that silence, we may choose to awaken during the hours of 2 and 5 A.M., some of the best hours for quietness. Then we can listen more easily to that which is less demanding.

Today I will withdraw from the loudness and busyness of daily life. In doing so I have a greater chance to hear an inner still voice. As I listen, what do I hear?

279. Tolerance

These are the times that try men's souls.
—Thomas Paine

When I try to control or manipulate others, I waste valuable energy, and I usually end up restless and aggravated. Yet when I am tolerant of others, I am free of the need to control and manipulate them. Tolerance is a key that opens the door to contentment.

Contentment comes from knowing that I don't have to expend my energy controlling those around me. They have their own destiny to live, as I have mine. Letting others follow their path in life without interference, I have more strength to follow my own path. My masculine energy is forward-moving; it helps me accomplish my goals. I misuse this power when I exert it to change someone else's life. When I direct my energy inward to fuel my own inner light, I naturally let go of my need to control others.

Today I am content to allow others to live their lives without interference from me.

280. Discipline

Without discipline we can solve nothing. Discipline is the means of human spiritual evolution.

—M. Scott Peck

Discipline has become a nasty word to some. Yet discipline is essential and worthy of praise. There is also something particularly masculine about it, which is part of its beauty. Scott Peck describes discipline as "a system of techniques of dealing constructively with the pain of problem-solving instead of avoiding that pain." He lists four techniques of discipline: delaying gratification, assumption of responsibility, dedication to the truth or reality, and balancing.

The kind of discipline a man follows influences who he becomes. There are many kinds of discipline. Some discipline is external, being enforced from outside, such as in the military. Other discipline is internal, emerging from the self. Interior discipline is a gift to be cherished. Every artist needs the discipline of his craft. For a relationship to endure, it must develop its own discipline, organic to that connection. Discipline is essential for spiritual exploration. Discipline can bring focus and concentration. The appropriate discipline can help bring the appropriate structure—in a life, an event, or a process. Discipline helps us achieve our goals without being distracted by peripheral events.

Today I will be aware of how I practice discipline—in my work, in my relationships, and in my expression of soul.

281. Compassion

The hidden treasure in the sufferings, sorrows, and pains of the world is compassion itself. Compassion is the heart's response to sorrow.
—Jack Kornfield

Compassion is saying "yes" to oneself, others, and life itself, in spite of obstacles and difficulties. Compassion can connect us to all that is, including other people, other life-forms, the universe. Compassion melts the false separation of ourself and others. Compassion engenders generosity —giving and letting go, rather than hoarding and holding on.

Compassion can transform pain. Finding meaning in life's difficulties can be arduous. Faced with the loss of a loved one or great tragedy, we may be tempted to the extremes of rage or passive withdrawal. Yet the same difficulties can lead to great compassion—an acceptance of even the most challenging realities, allowing them to connect us to others on the common ground of sorrow. Through our tears we can come to beauty and a connection to all that is, even death. Sorrow can open us to tenderness, mercy, and kindness.

Today I will have compassion for myself, accepting myself for who I am. I will extend that compassion to others, especially those in times of tragedy, sorrow, and need.

282. Truth

Whatever satisfies the soul is truth.
—Walt Whitman

I can read about truth. I can listen always for the truth in what others have to say. I can learn about truth by witnessing the lives of great souls whom I admire. But whenever I seek the truth from an outside source, I must be careful not to lose sight of the greatest truth—which is found within my own Self.

The actual experience of truth is felt only after many layers of my old ideas and beliefs have been peeled away. My truth is intimately connected to who I am and what kind of relationship I have with God. My truth is the strong and ever-expanding center of my own being.

Today I will seek my own truth by embarking on the inward journey of Self-discovery.

283. Humor

Man is the only animal that blushes. Or needs to.

—Mark Twain

Sometimes I get so caught up in the rush of my life that I don't take time to pause and look around at the humor of the situations I get myself into. I can get so serious and solemn, placing importance on such trivial events, that I drive myself crazy with worry. Most things in my life are only as serious as I make them.

If I can meet my life circumstances with a sense of humor and lightness, my troubles will seem less important and heavy. If I don't take myself too seriously, life will be a lot less overwhelming, and a lot more fun.

Where is the humor and laughter in my life today?

OCTOBER 10

*Not every act of kindness is an act of
caretaking.*
　　　　　—Heard at a Twelve Step meeting

A number of years ago a man was enter-
ing a hotel where a large conference was
being held. His hands were full of lug-
gage. As he approached the door, another
man stepped out to hold the door open for
him. He smiled and thanked the Good Sa-
maritan, grateful for the help. As he
walked away, he heard the man holding
the door mutter in self-disgust, "I'm such
a caretaker."

　　It is very important to take care of
ourselves. But to be sure we are not falling
into the delusion of caretaking the world
and everyone in it (as so many men do),
we must also be aware of how important
small acts of kindness are. We live in community with others, interacting with people all the time. Taking a moment to be
kind and courteous to another will not de-
plete us, provided we're taking good care
of ourselves. Rather, by staying flexible
and willing to change our agenda to uplift
someone else, we are contributing to a
smoother, more peaceful world.

*Today I will practice conscious consideration
for others.*

285. Ethics

Somewhere between my ambition and my ideals, I lost my ethical compass.
— Jeb Stuart Magruder

Most evil in this world is not done by evil men, but by men who have simply lost their way, who simply strayed, little by little, from their own values and beliefs. There is a shadow in each of us that feeds on our ambition; given free rein in our lives, it can overwhelm our best intentions. At first I may not see the little compromises I make to attain my goals. I may tell a small lie, and follow it with denial and justification. I ignore the feelings and concerns of others in order to get what I want. In this way, choice by choice, I become more self-centered, less aware that my actions clash with my deepest beliefs.

None of us is immune to the gradual erosion of our moral principles, the loss of our personal ethics. We must practice vigilance today and every day. By taking the time to do a personal inventory, talking to trusted friends who will be honest with us, staying clear and conscious of my values, we ensure that we do not fall into the kind of compromises that can ultimately hurt us and those we love.

Today I will take a personal inventory of my choices, my behavior, and my motives.

286. Edges

When we come to an edge we come to a frontier that tells us that we are now about to become more than we have been before.
— William Irwin Thompson

Men's work is the process of healing by reconnecting with the Deep Masculine. In doing this work, we men are invited to explore our edges. Some of these edges we respect by stepping back. Often, though, a man is emboldened to cross over the edge into a new way of being.

Some men lack adequate edges to protect themselves; too much of the outside world seeps in. They would benefit from constructing clear boundaries. Other men have more boundaries than they need at this time in their lives. They have grown but are still defending themselves along the edges defined in the past. Each of us comes with some baggage we are unaware of. That baggage can get rigidified into edges.

As men we have the choice to evolve and expand. We need to realize that we are always living in a new historical moment and can, at any point, extend the edges of our knowing, thinking, feeling, being, and doing.

Today I will explore the edges of my awareness, discovering which edges protect me and which shut me in.

287. The Body of a King

Living under the power of a bodiless king is a bad way to live.

—Robert Bly

In making the above remark, Robert Bly was probably thinking of his own father, no longer living, whose memory still seemed to control his movements from afar. Many of us, too, are discovering that we have been "living under the power of a bodiless king." We slowly realize that, not only is our emperor wearing no clothes, he doesn't even have a body! He remains in control through his spoken messages to us, through our memories and fears from boyhood. Many of these messages have become stale and empty, not at all the kind of vital food we need to nourish our lives.

We men are waking up to the fact that we have a body, too, not just a mind. The total Body embraces brain, brawn, and soul. Our body is a great gift, not merely a machine that transports our head around. The body is to be enjoyed, experienced, nurtured, and respected. Most of all, we need to allow the body to open to those who love us.

The king who acknowledges his body blesses those around him who want to crawl into his arms, hold his hands, sit in his lap, and cuddle with him. By remembering our "body wisdom," we become our own king.

Today I'll take care of my male body with all the love and devotion a good king gives to a loyal subject.

288. Hands

'Tis God gives skill,
But not without men's hands: He could not
*   make*
Antonio Stradivari's violins
Without Antonio.
                    —George Eliot (Mary Ann Evans)

My hands are the hands of a man. They are strong, and have built bridges, rockets, and temples. They are gentle, and have held children in their protective strength. These hands have fashioned toys and weapons; they have tilled the land, killed for food, and painted the reflected beauty of God. My hands are a wondrous extension of my body, an expression of the constant creator that lives within me, within every man.

My hands not only have the power to build, they also have the power to heal. The touch of my hands can bring comfort to those who suffer; the caress of my hands can soothe a troubled heart. My quiet touch can break the isolation that has so often separated me from other people.

Today, with respect and love, I will reach out my hand to a brother.

289. Baths

I have had a good many more uplifting thoughts, creative and expansive visions while soaking in comfortable baths . . . in well-equipped American bathrooms than I have ever had in any cathedral.
—Edmund Wilson

Baths are great, especially hot ones. To sit for a while in water can bring much pleasure. The pause for water can delight, refresh, and sustain. We can shed the day, or the night. Baths are a great time to be alone, to reflect, to touch oneself and feel the whole body. Hot baths can awaken—the body, the soul, memories. Baths can be creative, especially if you add oil or bubbles. It helps to give attention to those places where we are every day, including our bathroom.

In baths we lie down, which can induce deep relaxation at the end of the day, before sleeping. Afternoon baths can also help with naps and bring a time of reflection into the middle of the day. A good bath reduces muscle tension, expands the blood vessels and thus lowers blood pressure, and hydrates dry skin. Baths cleanse us, soothe us, and provide a place for singing or chanting. Some people make bathing into a relaxing ritual.

Water is gentle and soft, yet it has great power to transform. Baths can also be a social occasion—for a couple, family, or circle of friends. From the European spas to Japanese public baths to hot tubs, people are discovering the values of social bathing.

Today I will enjoy a good bath. I may want to record my thoughts and feelings.

290. Going Down

Mankind owns four things
That are no good at sea—
Rudder, anchor, oars,
And the fear of going down.
> —Antonio Machado (translated by
> Robert Bly)

Antonio Machado was a somber Spanish poet. He drew from his culture's rich appreciation of tragedy and the dark side of life. Some cheery people feel you always have to be happy. Such people fear "going down." Yet it is precisely in *going down* that we enable ourselves to come up and touch the heights of ecstasy. In our men's gatherings we have noted a connection between men's capacities to go into the depths and then rise to the heights.

Depression, according to Robert Bly, is when "we refuse to go down, so a hand comes up and pulls us down." Depression is not the same as grief, which is when we choose to go down. The gifts of descending can be substantial.

Today I will open myself to the importance of going down. When I descend, what do I encounter? What do I fear about going down? Perhaps I will find treasures that have long been hidden in the depths. I will remember that what goes down must come up.

291. Death

It is difficult to accept death in this society because it is unfamiliar. In spite of the fact that it happens all the time, we never see it.
—Elisabeth Kübler-Ross

I have hidden my eyes from the natural end of life. Out of fear and misunderstanding I have turned my back on death, secretly, irrationally hoping that it will never happen to me or to the ones I love.

But hiding from death only brings about more fear. Whatever I may believe will take place after my death, it is a certainty that someday my body will stop working and die. If, instead of turning away from this truth, I can look at it directly, I will cease fearing and denying it. Then I'm free to value what matters most —my inner life—and to accept my physical life as the temporary thing that it is.

Today I will care for my body well, and live my life to the fullest possible measure—not because I fear death, but because I love life.

292. Your Death

Have you built your ship of death, O have
*   you?*
O build your ship of death, for you will need
*   it.*

—D. H. Lawrence

We can do much to influence our death, by how we live our lives and by how we prepare for death. Ours is a death-denying culture. When we integrate death as a part of life, we can be better prepared for its inevitable arrival.

Imagine your death. How do you fear it might occur? How would you like it to be? As you think of your own impending death, does another death come to mind? Who was the person who died? Or perhaps it was an idea, an animal, a home, or something else that passed away, perhaps too early or unexpectedly. What is the worst thing that could happen to you as you imagine yourself dying? What is your greatest loss? What will you miss the most?

Now imagine your death as you would *like* it to be. Who else is there? Where does it happen? How old are you? What are you dying from? What do you want to say to your friends? What do you want to leave behind? Is there any particular music, poetry, or other art that you want as you depart? How do you want to be remembered? You may want to write your own obituary as you would like it to appear in the newspaper.

Today I will visualize my own death, as I would like it to be. I will allow myself to have whatever feelings emerge as I consider my own death.

293. Healing Myself Through Service

A sure way for one to lift himself up is by helping to lift someone else.
—Booker T. Washington

When I fall into depression, despair, or hopelessness there seems no way out of it. I feel stuck and helpless. These feelings eat away at my self-esteem; my soul feels frozen. The longer this goes on, the more isolated and lonely I feel, until even the thought of taking action seems overwhelming.

All is not hopeless, of course. I can take action. If I reach out to help another person, my feelings of isolation and helplessness are quickly shattered. I become free. Simply by taking my focus off my own troubles to offer service to another, my spirits are lifted. This simple and great gift is a miracle I can count on.

Today I will offer to help another person. Offering service ensures my ability to reach out during times of despair, and it also assures that I will have less of that despair.

294. Happiness Is an Inside Job

The foolish man seeks happiness in the distance, the wise grows it under his feet.
—James Oppenheim

Some days I wake up hell-bent on happiness. If I pause at those times, I usually notice that I've found it, and wonder how I got here. My happiness comes from what happens, and what I do with it. Happiness exists in what's happening now, not in my daydreams of what's going to happen some other day.

Wise souls in all ages have said the same thing: if I don't practice the art of finding my "happiness" right where I am, then nothing that changes outside me will *make* me happy.

Today I'll enjoy what happens as best I can, and accept all that takes place (both the easy and the difficult) as being full of potential joy.

295. Slowing Down

When you slow down, you begin to discover there is a silent awareness of what it is that you do not want to look at.
—Malidoma Some

When I'm running and racing, I don't have time to remember the woundedness and grief I have carried in my body for decades. Yet when I get off the fast track, pausing to take time for myself, the deeper issues begin to surface. I may shove these feelings out of my mind, until an illness lays me up, or the boss lays me off. In such moments, the process of healing begins.

By consciously slowing down on a regular basis, instead of waiting for a crisis to do it for me, I begin to remember my body again. I discover that, despite what I'd been taught, gentleness and silence are not my enemies. If I move too fast to feel through the grief, I'll miss the happiness, too. And while the process may be painful at times, it is this slowing down, this silence, that gives birth to joy and freedom.

Today I will not rush. By slowing down, I indicate my willingness to face the memories I have shoved out of my awareness. Not only can I survive these memories—I can be strengthened and delighted in the process.

296. Letting Somebody Else Win

There are some defeats more triumphant than victories.

—Michel Eyquem de Montaigne

At a certain point in a young boy's life, his father should let him win, let him be right. Whether the battle is physical or intellectual, it is a crucial threshold for the boy, who needs to become a man in his own eyes as well as in the eyes of his father. If a boy does not receive this gift, he may end up like his own father, harboring a destructive need always to be right, to be stronger, smarter, and wealthier.

We needed to win with our fathers. We wanted to win as a symbolic act of independence. To actually usurp our fathers would have horrified us. But the *symbolic* win is an act of greatness on the part of the father, his admission that he can bend for the sake of love. Such an act also allows the boy to take back the "God energy" he may have invested in his father, placing God first, and putting Dad back in perspective as a human being.

As men whose own sons and daughters prepare to enter adulthood, we can watch for an auspicious moment to step aside and let them win an argument, a chess game, a wrestling match. And every day we can let our children win our deep affection, something they will keep with them forever.

Today I'll meet myself and others with a new kind of compassion. When someone else really wants to be right, to be stronger or smarter, I'll let him win, just for the practice. In this way, I'll learn that humility does not diminish me.

297. Acceptance

No snowflake falls in an inappropriate place.
—Zen saying

Often, when a difficulty or calamity occurs, we feel it must have happened because it was "supposed to," that somehow it was what we needed, and that no matter how painful, it was in our own best interest in the long run. Sometimes we can see this truth so clearly, but at other times we fight and struggle against it. Years may pass before clarity arrives.

At the most difficult times in our lives, we can be drawn deep into ourselves. We reexamine our choices and our goals to check their integrity. Our "worst days" can help us return to what's most important. We may ask ourselves, "Why am I still doing what I've always done? Acting the same ways I always have?" Asking hard questions of ourselves is part of the work of growth, the real challenge.

All we know for sure, whether things are going well or not, is that we can't figure everything out mentally. We've tried and failed a thousand times. But we *can* know the truth that speaks to us quietly inside, and we can trust it.

Rather than try to "get all the answers down," I can accept the imponderable, even revel in it; I can learn to love the mystery.

298. The Practice of Knowing Nothing

The essence of knowledge is, having it, to apply it; not having it, to confess your ignorance.
—Confucius

One day I'll give up all judgments, all the things I thought I knew. Maybe I'll roll around like a red wheelbarrow, ready to be filled, unable to dump on anyone. I'll forget I know the world is round and discover for the first time that it is. I'll pretend I don't know the differences between men and women, so I can know the joy of finding them again. I'll let go of my old understanding of the word "duty" and let each day provide its own definition. Then "masculinity" will be a word I'll ponder without fear. With conviction I'll come near to the people I love; I'll look them right in the eyes to find out who they are. I won't ask either of us to "prove ourselves."

Today I'll practice keeping an open agenda. I'll practice knowing nothing. I'll let my wife, lover, friend, or child teach me about this life. And, because I need to know, I'll listen.

299. Nature

Earth's crammed with heaven,
And every common bush afire with God.
                    —Elizabeth Barrett Browning

When I take in the presence of nature, I feel wonder and awe. Standing on the shoulder of a mountain, or on the shore of a wild sea, helps me to place myself in a grand perspective. The natural glory of a star-filled night, the serenity of a calm and peaceful lake, can touch what is sacred in me. I wake to my own wild nature and spirit, and to my connectedness with all that lives. I recognize that, apart from all the "civilized" gadgetry with which I get involved, the lively rhythmic beauty of this earth is what sustains me. In the realm of this untouched beauty, I find my deepest Self.

Today I can honor the power of the elements by going to a place of natural beauty. Opening my mind and heart, I will allow myself to be touched by its grace.

300. Reclaiming Our Wildness

In the presence of nature a wild delight runs through the man in spite of real sorrows.
        —Ralph Waldo Emerson

These days many men are going back to the woods to tend wounds that will not stay hidden under the light of sun, moon, and stars. In the silence and safety that only a field, a stream, or a forest can provide, a deep healing naturally takes place. Our healing must be untutored and unstructured. To honor it, we strike out beyond the city limits to a place where we feel simple against the backdrop of the earth.

As boys, many of us took to the woods and came to know the trees, rocks, and grassy knolls as spiritual mothers and fathers, as friends. When we became men, though, we pulled away from the earth. We forgot the good heft of stone. We forgot that we were creatures of the land. We left the great rooms filled with sky, the chapels made of cedar and cypress, to seek out the sights and smells of the city. After our long estrangement from the earth, we need to return to the natural wonders now and then, to purify our vision, to partake in the daily ceremonies nature conducts.

Today I'll check in with the earth that holds me up. I'll see how long it's been since I took in the delight that the wild places create in me.

301. Volcanoes

*Volcanic mountains are always linked with
and aware of the larger networks of connected
forces beneath the surface of the earth. . . .
The strength of the fire element is needed
everywhere: in your bodies, in your smelter, in
the earth, in the sun.*

—Dorothy MacLean

Men can be volcanic and fiery. Volcanoes
represent a deep internal power. Dorothy
MacLean encourages us to recognize that
power in ourselves and dedicate it to the
whole, and also, she writes, "to be accu-
rately precise in the gift that power gives."
Seeing a volcano explode is the kind of experience one never forgets. The sky suddenly becomes full of red-hot light and
fire. Exploding with fire can be appropriate or inappropriate, depending on the situation and the people involved. But a man
should never give up his capacity to explode, because someday it may save his
life.

Being gentle and lightweight is not always sufficient; having the energy of a
volcano or a dragon can help move things.
The fire of volcanoes can help protect and
set limits. Volcanoes have an earthy wisdom. Volcanoes and explosions can have
great beauty to them. Appreciate that
beauty.

*How is your volcano? Have you tamed it?
Does it spout off too often, disrupting your
life? Or might you benefit from its fire?*

302. Warming Love

Warming love creates soul.
—Thomas Moore

As boys, many of us received a cold love from our fathers. The distance between us lowered the temperature and the angry words blowing between us became cold winds. The frigid looks we got from our fathers sometimes froze our very souls and bodies. The shame we felt for not being what they wanted seemed to trap us in a cave of ice.

Men are thawing out now. Our anger and our grief are fires that can cook up a warmer Soul. The cold family is now replaced by the men's group, the walks alone in the woods, the journal we write in, the support meetings we attend. A men's gathering is like a cauldron where thick, warm, nourishing Soul is made, and blessed, and shared.

Today I'll look for the kind of love that creates a warm Soul. And I'll let safe people sample this wounded but wonderful "Soul de jour."

303. Soul Friend

*Go off and don't eat until you get a soul friend,
because anyone without a soul friend is like a
body without a head.*

—Saint Brigit

The soul friend—what the Irish call an
anamchara—is a wisdom figure that helps
connect us to something that dwells in the
soul and beyond, to the transcendent. In
the Christian tradition of the fourth and
fifth centuries there were desert fathers
(*abbas*) and mothers (*ammas*) who sought a
special intimacy with God by going into
the desert wilderness away from the decay
of the city. These mystics became good
soul friends, spiritual mentors, or spirit
companions to others.

A soul friend is one who is mature,
compassionate, and respectful. We can go
to him to confess and know that what we
say will be held in confidence. He will
share our journey, allowing us to disclose
without judgment. He will help us discern
the movements of our soul. He is usually a
wise old man who is often quite worldly.
He may be firm or stern with us, as well as
playful. Or he may be a young boy
learned beyond his years. He may range
across many ways of being with us.

*Today I will connect with a soul friend. He or
she may be a familiar guide, or this may be the
beginning of a new relationship. Perhaps I can
make this connection in person, by phone, by
mail, or in my mind.*

304. Fatherhood

It's clear that most American children suffer too much mother and too little father.
— Gloria Steinem

There are many reasons why most of us grew up with a father who was absent either emotionally or physically. We have felt the wound of his absence, and we have suffered the consequences. But our suffering does not happen in a vacuum. Our whole society has been hurt by this father wound. We can learn from the mistakes our fathers made, by coming back into our families, by accepting our own feelings, by placing our work in its true perspective.

Today is different. I can be available to father my sons and daughters in a way that my own father could not be. I can guide them, teach them, and love them. The cycle of absent fathers can end with me.

Today I will stand up and take my rightful place as a father in my family, my community, and my world.

305. Masks and Mask-Making

OCTOBER 31

Masks are associated with change. . . . What they will mean, what they will do, what they will become when they are worn is not predictable. The mask is at once rigid and flexible.

—D. F. Pocock

Halloween is the time of year that our culture has reserved for wearing masks. Actually, we each wear many masks all year. We wear some of them when we face the public, others when we encounter a partner in bed. We can add to our collection as we see fit. Masks help us interface between the inner and outer worlds. Masks can help protect, especially that which is fragile. Masks are related to change and transition. They help us pass borders. They are connected with rites of passage and other ceremonies.

Men can create their own masks, using the same material surgeons use to make casts. This flexible material goes on the face wet and is taken off when it dries. These masks reveal something of a man's essence. They can be sculpted and painted, or decorated with feathers, leather, and other objects. A man may have a certain mask in mind as he creates —a boy, a wise old man, an animal, or perhaps his inner woman. Or the mask may just emerge. These outer masks can evoke inner characters and qualities, some of which are hidden. Some masks we choose; others choose us.

Do I have the masks I need? If not, I may want to fashion one today. I can simply look into a mirror and with my facial muscles transform my face into a mask.

306. Taking Off the Mask

NOVEMBER 1

Courage is resistance to fear, mastery of fear, not absence of fear.

—Mark Twain

As boys, some of us were so lonely that, to endure, we created ourselves like fictional characters. Through childhood and adolescence, all the way to adulthood, we carried these half-developed personas. We felt flat, like cardboard cutouts. These false characters allowed us to survive our pain, but it took a lot of energy to keep them performing. Were it not for the fact that most of us had an inner dictator ruthlessly directing the show, we would never have made it past the second act.

Now I slowly step off the stage. Taking a long, hard look at myself, I pull off the mask. It's painful to see how little of my real self is still intact.

Today, instead of creating a role to play, I'm creating a Soul with real character and integrity. Occasionally I may slip back into acting and delivering old, stale lines that never really worked. But I don't do it as often, and I can hear the difference. And there are more men in my life today who will gently remind me when I'm departing from my truth.

Today I'll slow down and stop performing. I'll look at why, when, where, and with whom I started acting a part instead of just living.

307. Death

Remember you are dying.
—Sign found in inns of the Middle Ages

Rather than being morbid, the essential message of this sign is, "Today you are alive." This wake-up call reminds us that life is a gift that we will not always have.

Death is the greatest mystery. Some people think of death as an event at the end of life. Yet life itself is a process toward death. Death is with us from the beginning. Birth and death are brothers. Death is not something contrary to or outside life; it is within life and ever-present. We are always dying. Plato says that all living is a preparation for death. Death defines life.

The death of a man's father, according to Freud, is the most important death in his life. When a father passes, the son can become aware that he is that much closer to the grave himself. Seen in the right light, that death can inspire us to become more alive.

Today I will reflect on death, imagining what it must be like. Will it bring peacefulness? Light? If the thought of death inspires fear, I will ask why, and go beyond my fear.

308. Angels

Life is saved by the singing of angels.
—Howard Thurman

Angels are always here among us. They are not so distant; they hover. Each angel has a name and its own way of being. Some are male, some female; sometimes they come without gender. Looking into the innocent eyes of a child, or the dark eyes of an old man, we may recognize the presence of an angel. Angels are messengers, connecting us to another world, a most ancient world. They can become guides to that world and its storehouse of knowledge. Their essential gift is one of relatedness.

Many of us have guardian angels, although we are usually not aware of them. If we are not, we may choose to work on developing their silent presence. Our task is to open our senses wide enough to perceive these special beings. Inviting them into our lives is a good beginning.

Angels arrive when I need them and call for their help. Angels support and bless, offering wisdom. They can also bring surprises. Today I will look for signs of angels hovering nearby.

309. Fathering Ourselves with Love

Children have more need of models than of critics.

—Joseph Joubert

I wake up and hear "the voice." I know whose voice it is; it doesn't belong to me. The tone is harsh, the words shaming, demeaning, degrading. It speaks of worthlessness, of laziness. The voice addresses a boy, not a man.

Many of us, as boys, received less-than-supportive messages from the men we loved, feared, and looked up to. Hundreds of times we heard, "You're no good." To silence that still-echoing voice, we have to repeat to ourselves hundreds of times, "You're worthwhile," "You're important," "You're precious," and "You belong here, just as you are." I'm determined not just to *know* the truth about my worth, but to *feel* it in my words, in my body.

Today I'll start telling myself the truth about myself. I'll tell the cruel voice to be silent.

310. Loving Tolerance

Only when we learn how to put up with ourselves can we arrive at a place of interior peace.

—Thomas Moore

Sometimes it takes years to realize that parts of our life aren't working as well as we had hoped they would. To make some changes, we've had to do some self-inquiry. It may take several more years to make real headway on those changes. But once our new behavior takes hold, it feels natural, even comfortable. A few more years go by, and we realize that some things about ourselves we can't change; they are a basic part of the way we are. At that point we see that *intolerance* of our own quirks was one of our biggest problems all along.

Self-tolerance is perhaps the most difficult thing any of us has to embrace on the healing journey. We can do the therapy, read the books, and share in men's groups. But accepting ourselves as we are is vital. We can't stay stuck in old concepts of perfection. There lies intolerance, and self-love goes out the window. Until we accept who we are, we can't become the person we are meant to become. We learn love by first practicing on *ourselves*.

Today I accept myself unconditionally. I trust that I will change in due time, but naturally, not by pushing myself harder.

311. Being the True Self

*In order to heal we must recognize our loss of
connection with three significant relationships
—with Source, Self, and others.*

—Jed Diamond

From the day of our birth until the beginning of our adult recovery journey, we
look for something or someone outside
ourselves to make us feel whole. As we
first entered the world, we also entered a
family that might have helped us discover
and celebrate our true Self, that innocent
being still connected to the Source. Instead
many of us were taught to live for others
and forsake ourselves. We learned that listening to and acting on our inner truth
was considered "selfish."

Buddhism teaches that we should
transcend the self or empty the self. Chris-
tianity teaches that the death of the self is
a high calling. But many of us are confused by both teachings. Because we had
never truly known ourselves to begin
with, we didn't have anything of our own
to transcend, nor to give up for something
greater.

Today men are discovering that it is
not a selfish act to find and be that Self.
Quite the opposite. By becoming my true
Self, just by being myself, I spontaneously
connect to that which is greatest in me,
and in others as well.

*Today I'll take steps to more fully discover and
develop my inner Self. What I really am, I can
know and trust.*

312. Delight and Wildness

I caught a glimpse of a woodchuck stealing across my path, and felt a strange thrill of savage delight, and was strangely tempted to seize and devour him raw; not that I was hungry then, except for that wildness which he represented.

—Henry David Thoreau

Men are too civilized today. We are too out of touch with those animal instincts that have enabled men to survive all these centuries. We are the descendants of those men, the ones who were wild enough to survive. Others, who lacked this wildness, fell to the side along the way. When men move away from wildness in the outer world, when we stop looking wild animals in the eyes, we lose contact with our inner wildness.

Too often, in search of safety and security, we isolate ourselves from that which would refresh and revitalize us—wilderness, where things are not controlled and tamed. It is important to abandon one's safety at times and venture into the unknown on adventures. Thoreau writes of "thrill," "delight," the temptation "to seize." These are wild feelings, too often suppressed in men today. Children know delight, until they are tamed. The world offers itself for our delight.

Today I will search for my wildness. Perhaps I can feel it in running after a wild animal. I will pursue that which delights me.

313. Safety and Wildness

What we want from each other most intimately . . . (is) wildness and safety, or a magical space that includes both.

—Robert Hass

Safety is talked about a lot these days in certain circles. Such talk can get to be too much, leaving out so much. Though safety is essential, especially for children, too much can inhibit growth. Safety can be a good beginning, but there needs to be more. Wildness can be an important ingredient added to safety that encourages growth, taking adults beyond their edges and into the unknown.

Wildness is that which is open and spontaneous. Too great an emphasis on safety is that we can lose vitality. Safety needs to be balanced with some risk-taking. "Forget safety," the ancient poet Rumi advises, "I have tried prudent planning for long enough. From now on, I'll be mad." Rumi prefers the joy of being on the edge and dealing with the unfamiliar.

Safety in our world is an illusion. At any moment, no matter how careful one has been, something unpredictable can happen. In fear of the unpredictable, some people become too tame.

Today I will develop my inner safety. With that security I will also extend myself and take appropriate risks.

314. Honoring the Inner Mysteries

When something is mysterious, it doesn't quite have a name.

—Ron Kurtz

In every man's body there are many subtle feelings that can't be described in words. They are nameless, though sometimes as they leave our bodies we can identify them through their mysterious sounds—groans, sighs, deep cries. These feelings can be powerful, expressed as guttural growls or high-pitched screams. And there are moments of such ecstatic delight that they can only be danced or drummed, if they are expressible at all.

My body is as mysterious as a mountain. What lies within me is often unnameable, exciting, sometimes frightening, and fun to discover. I don't need to solve my inner mysteries any more than I need to "solve" a river or a tree. Just acknowledging the mystery, knowing of it, enlivens me and gives me faith that I'm on a great adventure.

Today I won't force a name on to what I feel or what I utter. I'll just watch with respect as the mystery of my inner Self emerges.

315. Otherness

Your duty is to be, and not to be this or that.
—Ramana Maharishi

In the airport corridor, a slender, middle-aged man dressed in blue denim and brown corduroy, wearing Tony Lama boots and a big western hat, glances with respectful interest at the man waiting next to him, taking in the three-piece suit, the oxford shirt, the tie in a Windsor knot. The cowboy tips his hat to the gentleman. Both men know who they are and show no fear of the other's "otherness."

The man who is simply himself makes no apologies for it. None is necessary. He's free. He doesn't need to judge other men, or be concerned with their approval. This quiet confidence is not an Old West machismo, but rather a knowledge gained from going inside and discovering who we really are and then just being that. Why are men now moving toward greater consciousness? It's not that we're defective; it's just that we're awake now, able to feel curious and desirous of more of the good that life has to offer.

Today I'll forget the opinions of others. If I haven't yet fully understood who I am at my core, I'll begin right now. If I already know how to rest at my center, I'll enjoy the quiet strength and serenity that comes from honoring my Higher Self.

316. Decisions

God grant me the serenity
To accept the things I cannot change,
The courage to change the things I can,
And the wisdom to know the difference.
                                    —The Serenity Prayer

The Serenity Prayer is a useful guide in making decisions. It reminds me that I am not alone, that I can call on my Higher Power to aid me in my decisions. It also reminds me to approach my choices from a serene point of view. This is extremely important, because decisions made under stress and confusion often result in poor outcomes.

The prayer urges me to accept that there are situations in life over which I have no power. The best decision at these times is simply to understand that I don't have to do anything; I only need to accept what is. The prayer then goes on to recognize the courage it takes to change my unworkable ways of being in the world. True change requires commitment and perseverance. I accept the fact that, as part of my decision to change, I may be called upon to put forth a great deal of effort. Again I'm reminded that, every moment, I can ask my Creator for support, for the wisdom to make the best choice.

Today I will use the Serenity Prayer as a guide in at least one decision.

317. Problems

Problems do not go away. They must be worked through or else they remain, forever a barrier to the growth and development of the spirit.

—M. Scott Peck

Perhaps you are facing a problem—huge or small, new or old. Perhaps you would like to ignore and deny it, in hopes that it will vanish. It will not vanish magically. In fact, if you do not attend to it, it may grow larger. Today is a good day to attend to problems.

Problems can be multiple—financial, sexual, family. But good solutions are even more numerous. Every problem has more than one adequate solution and many paths toward those solutions. Embark on a path, even if it is not the best one; you can usually change. When men get together in men's groups or gatherings they often come with many problems— some they voice openly, others remain hidden. Sometimes a man thinks he is the only one with a certain problem. By being open to the sharing of problems, men can help each other the many paths to solutions. Knowing that others wrestle with similar problems can help break our isolation.

Today I will focus on a problem. I might allow another man to know of this problem, and together we will allow solutions to emerge.

318. Love

Love cures people—both the ones who give it and the ones who receive it.

—Karl Menninger

My ability to love is huge, encompassing, limitless. I can deeply love a friend, a child, or a lover. My love can be expressed in countless ways, sometimes tenderly and quietly, sometimes fiercely and protectively. The more freely I give love, the more freely I am able to accept it. This natural flow of love is the basis of all happiness and health.

Sometimes I may have difficulty expressing my feelings of love. This is not because I do not love, but because I may not always know how to communicate this powerful emotion. Every day I discover that my willingness to express love and my true manliness are closely linked.

Today I will express my love in my behavior and my words.

319. Friendship

What friends really mean to each other can be demonstrated better by the exchange of a magic ring or a horn than by psychology.
— Hugo von Hofmannsthal

A friend is a present you give yourself.
— Robert Louis Stevenson

My friendships are like precious gems or beautiful sunsets: they are natural wonders. If I take the time to savor them I discover that each of my friendships brings its own kind of joy. My friends grow along with me; we borrow strength from each other, offer experience and love. A true friendship thrives on respect and support.

We are in luck if we have the good company of men and women who are seekers, dreamers, and lovers of Spirit. Whether we're working together for a common purpose or just listening to each other's stories, we enjoy each other in countless ways. I can only guess at how much I've received from my friends.

Today I am thankful for the gift of real friendships.

320. Spending Time

To realize the importance of time is the gate of wisdom.

—Bertrand Russell

I tend to think I have plenty of time (and I do) to make mistakes, to learn, to heal. But somehow I don't seem to have enough time to love my life and my fellow travelers. I don't take time to express all the love I feel for others, to appreciate all the antics of children, to understand the wealth of grace that is inherent in my life. I want to feel that I'm having a great life, rather than rushing around trying to see all the sights in a cosmic tourist trap.

Yet when I do stop to watch the sun go down, standing alone as the sky pours out its wonders, I know I am a rich man. Spending my time well teaches me something important. While I'm here, I want to *live* these moments, understanding the value of each one.

Today I'll make time to touch the face of a loved one, look into the sky, get a hug, take a nap, say "I love you."

321. Restoring the Child

I'm looking for the face I had before the world was made.

—William Butler Yeats

A playful child lives within every man. There is a smile that comes to our lips now and then, the same smile that blossomed on the face of the infant we used to be. That smile says the child's still in there!

Our inner child may be hiding, waiting until he feels safe enough to whisper his secrets in our ear, to come out in the open, to put that smile back on our face.

It's our job, our duty and pleasure now, to make room in the body and in our life for this little boy. We can provide the feeling of safety he needs to make an appearance. We can keep the company of safe people, creating hallowed places where the child will not be shamed, shunned, or shut down. When this child knows he is welcome, he will emerge.

Today I'll look at where I go and what I do from the viewpoint of that boy who's still inside me. If I haven't done so already, I'll make a safe place for him. I'll listen to his secrets, and stay with him no matter how he feels.

322. Caught!

I'm caught in this curling energy! Your hair!
Whoever's calm and sensible is insane!
—Rumi

The thirteenth-century poet Rumi founded the Whirling Dervishes—a Sufi group that dances to ecstasy. He composed poems while whirling; his works have an unmistakable ecstatic quality. The words are sparse, the meanings full. Rumi offers a good antidote to being overly serious. When we are too serious we fail to get caught in the great energies that pass through our bodies and environments.

Men dancing with other men is common in traditional cultures, but in America we have been programmed to dance only with women. A few men get the point, and get caught up in a male energy that can carry them off to another delightful world, as happened to Zorba the Greek when he danced. Being caught up can be quite healthy. The ecstasy that Rumi describes is what some people today seek through alcohol and other addictive substances. In his dance, Rumi reveals a path toward spirit that is free of addiction.

What would I like to get caught up in today?
What energy could I benefit from being involved with right now? I will imagine a scene in which a person, thought, feeling, or process takes me away.

323. Obsessive Thinking

The power of memories and expectations is such that for most human beings the past and the future are not as real, but more real than the present.

—Alan Watts

Often I am not aware of myself, or of what I'm doing. I am thinking (often worrying) about the future, or reliving the past. Letting my mind carry on like this can become obsessive and self-destructive. Like many other men, I was taught to look outward, toward projects, people, and material goals rather than inward, to know my experience and to find out who I am.

Today I don't want to cover up my life with irrelevant thoughts. I choose to observe my inner experience. To cherish my life as it unfolds is my greatest occupation.

Today I will give time to the experience of my inner self.

324. Intellect and Identity

We should not make the intellect our god; it has, of course, powerful muscles, but no personality.

—Albert Einstein

For centuries, our self-esteem as men has been determined not only by how brave we were but by how well we hunted and then later by our intellectual ability. We still spend too much time exalting our brain, giving it far too much power in our lives. In the process, we've forgotten our intuition, our "native knowing."

Our dads, very intelligent men in many ways, sometimes would say to us, "I don't understand why you have so much trouble with your relationships. You're a smart man, you've read all those books. You ought to be able to figure things out and make your life work better." Of course, calling on intellect is not always the answer, because as long as our bodies are full of unfelt and unexpressed emotions, our thinking is usually not very clear or precise.

Today I know I need all of my human attributes: to go along with my powerful brain, I need my inner wisdom, the help of others, sometimes therapy, sometimes a group of supportive men, sometimes a simple afternoon with a small child. I want to be all of me, to feel, talk, touch, listen, laugh, grieve, and forgive, as well as be reasonable.

325. Men and Money

A wise man should have money in his head, and not in his heart.

—Jonathan Swift

For many men, money is a mystery. But most often we try to pretend we have more than we do, or that we don't really need much. At the very least, we pretend we understand it and that we've got it under control.

Most men are afraid that there's not enough money to go around. We were taught to hold on to our money in a fearful way, as if it were all that stood between ourselves and despair. Others grew up feeling that money was the most, perhaps the only, important thing in the world to their parents. Such men may purposely avoid becoming financially stable, and silently say to themselves, "See what they did to me; I can't make it in the world." Or they adopt the message, "If I make a lot of money maybe they'll finally be proud of me."

Some of us are afraid to tell other men how much money we have. We remember our fathers' taboo against talking about finances in concrete dollar figures. We remember how, once we grew too big to be physically overpowered, our dads used money to overpower us. We remember our feelings of shame, and we want to do things differently.

Today I'll explore the mystery of money—how I've been hurt around money, how I've been crazy with it, or afraid of it, or vain from hoarding too much. I'll work on seeing money as a tool for the exchange of love in service, a tool that can play a part in building better lives for all of us.

326. Reflecting on the Self

A man of knowledge is one who knows his own essential nature.

—Gurumayi Chidvilasananda

What a man really has, is what is in him. What is outside of him, should be a matter of no importance.

—Oscar Wilde

A man, upon meeting another man for the first time, asked a simple question: "Who are you?" The reply was immediate: "I'm a carpenter." The first man smiled and said, "That's what you do, but who are you?" The other replied, a little more slowly, "I'm a seeker of truth." The first man said, "That's what you're doing, but who are you?" Now a little angry and defensive, the other said, "I am a man." The first replied, "That's what sex you happen to be, but who are you?"

For every answer he gave, the first man re-asked the question. The more he pressed for an answer, the angrier the other got. Finally he had had enough and shot back, "Who are *you*?" The first man smiled, shrugged his shoulders, and said, "I'm not sure, but I've been trying to find out for the past ten years."

We play many roles—husband, father, friend, citizen, to name a few. Sometimes we need to stop and ask, "Who am I?" We may not get a definite answer, but the very act of asking seems to bring us around to our center. We gain by wondering about the real "I," the one who is not limited to any of the roles we play in life.

Today I ask myself, "Who am I?" Clarity comes from seeing how many identities I have, and discovering what is most important.

327. Taking Risks

Dare to be wrong and to dream.
                    —Friedrich von Schiller

My dream was to write a book. So I bought a typewriter and some paper, set up a small writing room in my house, and quit my job. Day after day I sat at my desk and looked at the pile of blank paper. Nothing happened. Not a word. The days strung out into weeks, the weeks into months. My dream and my reality were not matching up! As the months passed and my funds got low, I began to think I'd been a little hasty in quitting my job. I felt I'd made a big mistake, and that my dream was turning sour.

Finally my money ran out, so I put the blank paper away, covered up the typewriter, and went back to work. I felt defeated; I thought my dream of writing was over. But the project wasn't a complete failure: I had learned that sometimes my dreams and plans don't work out in exactly the way that I expect. I had also learned a great deal from trying something completely new, even if things hadn't gone the way I'd imagined them. Three years later I tried again to write the book (this time I didn't quit my job!). At this sitting, six of my books have been published, with more to come, I hope. And, for now, I still have my day job.

Today I will dream, and perhaps I will even risk putting my dream into action.

328. The Art of Gratitude

Gratefulness in the character is like fragrance in the flower.

—Hazrat Inayat Khan

When our worries suddenly outnumber our joys, when our thoughts become hurried and unfocused, we can stop what we're doing. Every moment carries small surprises: the movements of a spider traversing the windowsill, the wind blowing leaves in spirals in the air. Our lives are full of gifts, if we will see them: we have our bodies, our breath, our beliefs. We have a private collection of memories and dreams. We have the support of the earth under our feet, the support of our minds as we travel the past, the present, and the future. To turn inward to appreciate these wonders is the practice of *gratitude*, a nearly lost art.

Today I'll practice gratitude. By remembering what I've been given, I'll discover new treasures within myself.

329. Stories and Storytelling

Stories are medicine.
—Clarissa Pinkola Estés

Storytelling is an excellent way of caring for the soul. It helps us see the themes that circle in our lives, the deep themes that tell the myths we live.

—Thomas Moore

"Once upon a time, a long, long time ago" are familiar words. They cue the unconsciousness that we are going to the storytelling world—a place full of imagination and fantasy. Your inner child dwells within that world. Did your parents tell you stories before you went to bed? Storytelling for adults is returning as an art form and as a tool for healing, teaching, and spiritual growth.

Hearing old stories retold and telling our own personal stories can assist the Deep Masculine to emerge among a group of men. In many men's groups and at many men's gatherings, participants tell their personal stories, sometimes in the third person, rather than using the "I." We tell our stories as myths, beginning, "Once upon a time, a long long time ago, there was a boy. . . ." Telling one's own story in this way removes the ego and allows for new parts of the self to emerge.

Today I will tell or listen to a story. It may be my own personal story or one of the ancient stories. I will allow myself to listen deeply.

330. Leaning

I see when I walk how well all things
lean on each other . . .
        . . . then I understand
I love you with what in me is unfinished.
I love you with what in me is still changing.
                                    —Robert Bly

Trees lean on each other, making forests. Dirt leans into more dirt, making earth. Piglets lean into each other, merging energies. People lean on each other, making couples and community.

Some people lean too much, failing to stand upright on their own two feet and becoming dependent. They can drag us down. Others fear any leaning, because they associate it with weakness. "Don't lean on anyone" is a spell cast on some boys as they grow up. "Stiff upper lip" and "You can't depend on others"—such spells keep us men isolated, as if we were stones or islands rather than creatures given to leaning on each other. It is important to break the spells that were cast on us to keep us away from other people, including other men.

Leaning toward the right tree or person is key. Some trees are too young, too old, or too weak to hold your weight and would buckle. By the same token, some people collapse when you come toward them with any strong emotion. Others respond in ways that can deepen the connection.

Today I will find someone or something to lean on. I will let that someone or something hold my weight and any burden I may be carrying. I allow myself the comfort of sharing my weight.

331. Fathering

Women, it's true, make human beings, but only men can make men.

—Margaret Mead

For a long time our culture has encouraged us men to take a backseat in the work and play of child-rearing. We have focused our energy and time on seeking money, becoming successful, and trying to provide the best for our families. We have suffered, our children have suffered, and our culture has suffered from our absence as nurturing and guiding fathers.

Men need a uniquely male perspective that can only be taught to them by other men. Without exposure to men who care for them, spend time with them, and love them, boys miss an essential element in growing up. They miss learning to become men from real, live, flesh-and-blood males, and they turn to the unreal characters on film and television to fill the gap.

Even if we do not have children, or our children are grown, we can still fill the role of father for boys who lack a positive male influence. I only need to open my eyes; life presents me with many opportunities to serve. We can give our time and attention to these boys in need. If we have children of our own, we can consciously choose to make special time for them, to give them our best.

Today I will focus my energy and time on fathering.

332. Control

The ego and the soul vie to control the life force.

—Clarissa Pinkola Estés

Control is a two-edged sword. Without control one cannot survive. If we do not control our own lives, others will volunteer to take over. If we give up our power, someone else may assume it for us. Children are taught bladder control, tongue control, and control of the emotions. Each man must be in control of his life to be adequately productive, successful, and joyous.

The appropriate need to control oneself can expand to become a debilitating need to control others and one's environment. Such people are not fun to be around. They always have to be in charge. Trying to control others—either loved ones or people not so close—can be very problematic. It can lead to fights and even wars. Finding the right balance of control and surrender is key.

Feeling safe enough to abandon our need to control can be refreshing. If we always have our guard up, trust cannot develop. We lose spontaneity, vitality, and the pleasure of surprise if we are always in control. Creativity often comes when we relinquish control. Once we abandon the illusion that we can always control ourselves, others, and the environment, we open ourselves to unique possibilities.

Are there areas of my life where I exercise too much control? How might I give up that control today? What might make you feel more willing to share that control with others?

333. A Clouded Heart

Who never ate his bread in sorrow,
Who never spent the darksome hours
Weeping and watching for the morrow
He knows ye not, ye heavenly powers.
          —Johann Wolfgang von Goethe

There are days when the sun is hidden, when I look to the four directions and see only clouds. There are days when my strength, my smile is hidden from view, days when I'm needy, when I feel heavy and hurt.

When I'm feeling cold, confused, and small, I can take care of myself by sharing my pain with another person I trust. In this sharing I won't leave out the details, thinking they're insignificant or boring. I will not "act tough," "keep a stiff upper lip," or "pull myself up by the bootstraps." I have worth even when I'm not smiling or taking care of others. To share my sadness and confusion requires strength, courage. Like the sun, I don't always have to shine.

Today I will completely accept the clouds.

334. Stars

I feel above me the day-blind stars
waiting with their light. For a time
I rest in the grace of the world, and am free.
                                    —Wendell Berry

We men need contact with stars to help us understand our place in the universe. In many industrialized parts of the world, especially cities, it has become difficult or impossible to see stars at night. Stargazing is best done in rural areas, where there are fewer people, less pollution, less artificial light. After a few days there, we can feel better. Stars feed us in ways we can only partially understand.

Looking upward to the sky, which is always there, can expand our vision. Stars enable us to realize how large life is and how expansive the universe is. Stars enable us to imagine. They provide unique light that offers perspective on life here on the Earth. Stars make patterns in the sky that help us understand the great order underlying the cosmos. Not seeing the stars deprives us. The night—from which many contemporary people hide—has much to offer us. Always there, though not visible in the daytime sky, stars miraculously appear at night, providing dim light and bright guidance to those who know how to follow their direction.

If you are where you can see stars, notice them tonight. If not, consider finding a place—it may be only a short drive into the country—where city lights do not block out the stars.

335. The Mature Soul

> . . . I love to contemplate
> The mature soul of lesser innocence,
> Who hath traveled far on life's dusty road.
> —Henry David Thoreau

Some men have a certain look about them that reveals they have weathered life's storms. And that they have caused a few storms themselves. Sometimes it is a look in the eyes. Or a curve of the mouth. Or the way the features of the face come together. Not exactly a guilty look, but certainly no pretense to innocence.

Such men seem to be full. When a man steers his life with his own hands, those hands are bound to get dirty. Such men can be seen in the streets of Puerto Rico, in train stations in Scotland, on ranches in Canada, indeed in most places in the world, if we would open our eyes. Great mystery exists in those mature souls. Stories reside in them. Just gazing upon such men can be enjoyable.

Today I will go out and find a mature man. Somewhere near where I live there is such a man. I may want just to be around him. To look at him. Or talk to him.

336. Enchantment and Belonging

The view of nature which predominated in the West down to the eve of the Scientific Revolution was that of an enchanted world. Rocks, trees, rivers, and clouds were all seen as wondrous, alive, and human beings felt at home in their environment.

—Morris Berman

We belong—all of us, you and I, and all the creatures: birds, bugs, and everything. We were all meant to be here—together. We each have a place and a part—some big, others small. Men are not outside nature but an integral part of it. We are in constant exchange with everything. We are always giving and receiving, taking and discarding, taking in and putting out, holding and letting go. Our eyes connect us to all that is, much of which we can touch. It is all alive.

The scientific view of the world has restricted our vision, causing us to submit everything, even mystery, to scientific evaluation. Such evaluation can strip the world of enchantment. When we imagine other creatures and forms of life as having souls, then a connection is possible. No longer do we see ourselves as separate from and better than other forms of life. We can re-enchant the world with mystery and meaning.

Today I will feel my connection to rocks, trees, rivers, and clouds. If I cannot see them, I will imagine them. I will find as still a place as I can in nature, even if it is only a small amount of grass, then allow my imagination to unfold a story in that place. I am connected. I do belong.

337. Our Fathers

The longer I live the more keenly I feel that whatever was good enough for our fathers is not good enough for us.

—Oscar Wilde

Many of our fathers toiled in factories, fields, corporations, and the military. They were ranch hands, riveters, doctors, and shop owners. Whatever their work was in the world, they lived and worked by a standard that was forged by the times of their lives and their personal circumstances.

Times have changed; standards for life and work have evolved. For good or bad, our world is very different from that of our fathers. We cannot judge ourselves by their accomplishments or their standards. We can only measure ourselves against the yardstick of our own values and circumstances.

Today I can honor my father's accomplishments without using them to measure my own.

338. The Guest

Listen, my friend,
there is one thing in the world that satisfies,
and that is meeting with the Guest.
              —Kabir (translated by Robert Bly)

The Guest. Who is this Guest? He could be a friend, or a stranger. Or the Divine Guest who arrived to wrestle with Jacob in the Old Testament. Or an unfamiliar feeling. Welcome them all, the poet Kabir advises. The Guest can surprise and satisfy. When we are too rigid we keep the Guest out, in fear that he may rob us or eat our food. The Guest can break rigid patterns and leave us refreshed. The Guest represents the unknown, the unexpected, someone outside ourselves and our usual circle. His arrival can bring great change. Preventing his entry can preserve a necessary boundary, or it can block important growth. The choice is ours. When we are ready for the Guest, he can expand our capacity for receptivity, compassion, and love.

Men can benefit from more hospitality to each other. In certain cultures—such as ancient Greece—receiving a stranger as a guest and treating him with kindness and generosity was a sign of good breeding. The chief Greek god, Zeus, was the god of guests; he would sometimes disguise himself and walk among the people to see who would receive him. Receiving men, even those unknown to us, into our homes can enrich us in powerful and satisfying ways.

Today I will let the Guest arrive, allowing him to offer any gifts he may have.

339. Death of a Loved One

I remembered the times we had together when she was well . . . what it felt like to hold her, to make love with her, to wake up with her, to eat with her, to keep house with her, to argue with her, to live with her, to grow with her. . . . I also remembered how she died.
— Lewis Tagliaferre

An uncle once told his young nephew how important it is to put one's hands on the hands of the dead. At the time, this strange remark did not mean much to the boy, but he remembered it years later when the uncle died.

When the nephew arrived for the funeral, he entered the room quietly. The strong presence of his uncle's vitality filled the room. The nephew stood at the door for a while, awash in memories—playing cards with the man; stacking hay. It was hard to imagine this big, robust, vital, so-alive man now dead. Some time passed before the nephew could move toward the casket to look at the body, finally to touch him. His first feeling was not of cold, as he had expected, but of softness and a strange warmth. Then he felt a surge of power—moving from the uncle's hands into his.

A passage occurred in this exchange, from an older man to a younger man. Today, when the man finds himself in difficult moments, he recalls that powerful impulse—the final gift from a beloved uncle.

Do not be afraid of the dead. Touch them.

340. Toughness

Pray for a tough instructor,
to hear and act and stay within you.
    —Rumi (translated by Coleman Barks)

The ancient poet Rumi does not say a mean instructor; he says a tough one. Such teachers can "stay within." Toughness and kindness are not necessarily contrary. The first dictionary definition of toughness is "strong or firm, but flexible." The branches of certain trees, such as willows and bamboo, possess strength, firmness, flexibility, toughness. Be like such a branch—knowing when to hold and when to bend.

    Being tough—but not brittle or mean—can help us deal with life's inevitable ordeals and obstacles. Some people fall when pushed. The tough ones rise to meet challenges.

Getting to know some men is tough, but the journey can be well worth it.

341. Youth

Youth is wholly experimental.
— Robert Louis Stevenson

Boys and young men have a need to explore and to experiment. It's how we learn about life, develop values, and become compassionate men of self-respect and self-love. Boyhood is marked by a host of near-catastrophes, requited and unrequited loves, mysterious developments— all underscored by an ever-present hope for the future.

I must give the younger men and boys in my life enough room to make their errors, to find their own way. I can be there for support, or to provide a safe place to return to, but they must make their mistakes without judgment or interference from me. I can teach them through my experience, but I cannot *give* them my experience.

As a man, I can look back on my youth with fondness for the innocent adventurer I was. Remembering, my eyes open wider, my heart expands, and I feel the awe of that time. Everything was new; everything beckoned. As a man, I promise myself not to lose this great sense of exploration, and not to dampen it in others.

Today I will stay out of the way of my younger brothers, and allow "youthful folly" to take its course.

342. Resisting Judgment

Judge not thy brother!
There are secrets in his heart that you might
weep to see.

—Egbert Martin

It is easy to judge others by their actions, without taking the time to understand their inner suffering. Labels are an easy way out of caring. One man is labeled a "criminal" because he killed someone, another man is a "monster" because he molested a child. Yes, their *behavior itself* is horrible, inexcusable. But when we shirk the effort of knowing and caring about their suffering, about the root of their violence, we make it easier for such violence to continue in the world.

So often I have acted out of pain and fear, avoiding rather than accepting the challenge of understanding and compassion. We all need love to heal our wounds. To resist judgment is a deep form of love.

Today I will look beyond the behaviors and actions of those who have been labeled "cruel" or "hopeless." I will try to see their pain and suffering as though it were my own.

343. Living It

Slow down and enjoy life. It's not only the scenery you miss by going too fast—you also miss the sense of where you're going and why.
—Eddie Cantor

Years ago a man drove across most of the United States. Although he had no reason to hurry, he raced on anyway. That was the way he lived back then: rush, rush, rush. When he arrived at his destination, he had driven almost eighteen hundred miles in two days. He hadn't rested, and had only eaten while stopping for gas. He remembered nothing about his trip, as if he had passed through it all in a daze. He had spoken to no one. And he missed really seeing this vast country, the land's changing character. Through his grim determination to "get there fast," all he saw was gray highway and yellow lines.

Several years ago he again drove nearly eighteen hundred miles, but this time he took seven days. He looked at the countryside. He got a better sense of the land by getting out of his truck and walking around. He spent time in truck stops talking to other travelers. He thought deeply about why he was leaving his home of eighteen years. He thought about his new home and what it would be like to live there. Taking in the wonder of this beautiful land, he grieved the loss of his old home, and savored the excitement of the unknown. Years later he still remembered that second trip well, because he had enjoyed it. He had taken his time, and so he had experienced—and learned from—what was happening.

Today I will become conscious of what is lost when I hurry through life. I will slow down, letting myself experience what happens.

344. Relating to the Past

*The true past departs not; no truth or goodness
realized by man dies, or can die; but all is still
here, and, recognized or not, lives and works
through endless changes.*
　　　　　　　　　　　—Thomas Carlyle

Many of us drag the bleached bones of our
past with us into every moment, every
new encounter. We carry our woundedness from childhood and old relationships.

　　Other people can't always see the
burden we lug, and so are often completely baffled by our behavior. They tell
us we "should put the past in the past,"
"let sleeping dogs lie," that it's all just
"water under the bridge." But until we
can *feel* that past, we will be stuck in it.
Thus the past becomes the present. The
dogs won't sleep; they howl and chase us
in our dreams. The water that was supposed to pass under the bridge rises up
and floods our relationships with misun-
derstandings.

*Today if the past rises up in my path, I'll deal
with it. I'll surrender to its demands to be
heard, trusting that I'll come out more alive
than ever.*

345. Tradition

Tradition does not mean that the living are dead: it means that the dead are living.
—Harold Macmillan

We owe so much to the men who have come before us. Their lives laid the groundwork, the foundation for the present. Due to their wisdom and strength, we can step forward into the future. We all stand on someone's shoulders. We are not only indebted to the "great" men, the famous men, but also to those quiet men who, with persistence and vision, forged a simple tradition of spiritual values for us to follow. These men are alive in our actions and in our hearts.

Throughout our lives, so many men teach us, giving us the best they have to offer. This is the greatest tradition, the passing on of wisdom and values from one generation to another. Due to the generosity of these men, we ourselves have much to share.

Today I will honor the men who have taught me, who nurtured me and gave me their best so that, in my turn, I could pass it on.

346. Sharing

To meet at all, one must open one's eyes to another; and there is no true conversation, no matter how many words are spoken, unless the eye, unveiled and listening, opens itself to the other.

—Jessamyn West

Who do I talk to? Are there several men I can bare my soul to, who will listen to me without judgment? Do I talk to someone regularly about what is going on in my life and how I feel about it? These are important questions. Most of us were taught to live lives of isolation, walled off from the support of other men. When we were growing up we learned not to trust men with our feelings. It was okay to talk about sports, jobs, hunting, and other *activities*, but not about our inner life. For that reason it can be hard to learn to trust other men, and to risk talking to them about what we're feeling. But the effort is well worth it.

Sharing our hurt, grief, joy, and love with other men opens up a part of the heart that may have been walled off for many years. Behind that wall of distrust we may find parts of ourselves we did not know existed, a masculine sensitivity and depth that might astound us. Through sharing feelings we become connected to other men, and the isolation lifts. It's easy for the wall to be rebuilt, of course. All we have to do is stop sharing and begin to isolate again. But most of us wouldn't trade this new sense of depth and connectedness for anything.

Today I will make contact with another man by sharing my feelings and experiences.

347. Destiny

The whole secret of a successful life is to find out what it is one's destiny to do, and then do it.

—Henry Ford

From the time we were born, throughout childhood and on into adulthood, we were given messages from parents, teachers, and friends about what we "should do" with our lives. When we tried to follow these outer messages, instead of trying to understand our own destinies, we often ended up unfulfilled and confused.

To find our personal pathway through life, we need to enter the world of imagination and dreams. It's a place that lies beyond the influence of others, that only we can enter, because we create it. Only through using our own natural wisdom can we find our personal destiny. There are many ways to enter this place of dreams and imagination. Some enter by writing in journals, some by solitary walks and contemplation. Each of us must find the way that best suits him.

Today I will explore the inner world of dreams and imagination, so that I might discover my destiny.

348. Letting Go

Each person is born to one possession which outvalues all his others—his last breath.
                                        —Mark Twain

We all become attached to the things that make up our lives. Spouses, children, jobs, our looks, skills, possessions. We often believe that this "stuff" is who we are.

On 3×5 cards, write the seven things, people, or self-concepts that are the most important to you and number them in order of importance. Your list might include family members, career, friends, possessions, God. Twice a day for the next three days, reflect on the contents of the cards. You may wish to shift the ranking of the cards or change the items listed. On the third evening conduct a "letting go" ceremony. After reflecting one last time, begin with the lowest-priority card; say "I let go of this attachment" and then burn the card. What do you feel when letting go of this part of yourself? Repeat with the remaining six cards.

When finished, ask yourself, "Who am I without all of these important things in my life?" Your answers will help you understand who, at your core, you really are.

Today I will consider my attachments to the people and things in my life.

349. Great Souls Among Us

There are men who wield power without pride, who are rich but simple in their ways, who are learned but have no arrogance. They are divine spirits in human form.

—Baba Muktananda

He was a carpenter of simple words, with a scruffy manner and rough appearance. Yet he possessed a deep wisdom that came from a lifetime of experiences. In his seventies, he was still pounding nails, still driving his beat-up pickup truck. He always had time to listen to another guy, no matter how long he'd talk or what he'd say. He would nod, smile, and let the guy know that everything was going to be all right. Through his example of patient acceptance, he guided many men over the years.

Men and women of such divine spirit are mostly quiet people who stand in the background of our lives, guiding us with respect and gentle humility. They go about their daily lives with an easy grace, without drawing attention to their wisdom. To benefit from what they offer, I must listen with a finely tuned ear, letting go of preconceived ideas of who is wise, who is strong, who possesses skill. With a new vision unhampered by prejudice, I must look for these souls everywhere. I must look past their habits and their physical appearance to see the kind of work they do in the world.

Today, by looking for them in unexpected places, I will find these men and women of divine spirit.

350. Hunting and Communication

DECEMBER 15

Well-timed silence hath more eloquence than speech.

—Martin Farquhar Tupper

Long before men lived in urban settings, we lived on farms and in the country. Before that we lived in the wilderness. We developed skills to survive in those environments. Men went out to hunt together. Those who talked or made noise as they moved ran the risk of being eaten by the wild animals; they starved and their families perished. But those who were quiet got the wild boars. These men communicated with each other through signs and gestures. So let's be easy on the men who are not so quick to verbalize. We are all descendants of these strong, silent, successful hunters who brought the bacon home.

Imagine if your life and the lives of your family depended on your capacity to be quiet and hunt for a wild animal, one that preferred to eat you. Allow your imagination to construct a story. Such stories can be healing, helping us to integrate our inner realities with outer realities. The capacity of men to communicate is great. We can communicate deeply with those close to us, with others more distant, and with our inner selves. Though we may experience obstacles to communication, it is possible to break through and connect through word, deed, and body.

Much of male communication is nonverbal— how we act and what we do. Male modes of communication are valuable and even mysterious. A pause or gesture can mean much. Today I celebrate the many ways I communicate about myself and my maleness.

351. Coaches

Rockne wanted nothing but "bad losers."
Good losers get into the habit of losing.
                    —George E. Allen

Coaches can be important, not only for teenagers and not only in sports. A coach is a kind of mentor, one who can help us in many areas of life. He knows about the nature of certain things—such as teamwork. Coaches teach us about our bodies and how to strengthen them and use them. Some men's groups have drumming coaches, men who are further along than the others and who help the group keep the beat.

Is there anyone coaching you now? Could you benefit from coaching? If so, go and find a good coach. Are you coaching someone? It can be a great experience, in either role. Do you remember a really good coach whom you had? He probably gave you good attention and somehow inspired you. What were some of his qualities you admired? You can internalize those qualities when you work with others.

Is there someone whom I could coach? Someone who needs my coaching?

352. Complaining

We (can) know soul in its complaints: when it stirs, disturbed by neglect and abuse, and causes us to feel pain.

—Thomas Moore

Complaining has its place. If we have a legitimate complaint but do not express it clearly and directly, it is likely to come out anyway, in confused and sometimes harmful ways. Or it may stay in and damage the body. Breaking enforced silences can be life-enhancing.

Complaining can change things. If you hurt, express it. If someone hurts you, communicate that. Complaining as a daily practice can wear our friends down, whereas appropriate complaining allows us to clarify what we feel and think. Sometimes we complain because we want things to change. Other times the sheer release of our complaints is enough. Knowing how to complain and whom to complain to are key. Don't waste this energy on the wrong person.

Men have a lot to complain about, as individuals and as a group. Men are channeled into certain roles and kept from others. Men die eight years earlier than women in this society. Many men are unable to voice how they feel damaged by our society. Voicing those complaints can help us individually and as a group to improve our lives.

Today I will allow myself permission to complain, to say what needs to be said. I will move beyond whatever shame or politeness might restrict me.

353. Names

The sound of your name is song enough.

—Rumi

Your name is important. Your name carries your lineage; your ancestors are present in it. What echoes do you hear in the sound of your name? Pride? Shame? Is it your real name, the one your soul responds to? Do you have other names? Perhaps a nickname, or a name from childhood. Or a name in another language. Names in other languages can evoke different personas. If you have other names, say them now.

There is a naming ceremony men can do when they meet in groups. Each man comes to the center of the circle and says his name, as much of it as he chooses. Then together the community of men echoes his name—three times. Listening to our names being uttered ceremonially by men can be an initiation. In this ritual we might also evoke the names of those who have passed away, that we may remember them, or those who are suffering, that we may comfort them. Saying a person's name out loud in a group can focus that group's concern.

Today I say my name out loud, at least three times. I listen to the echoes of my name that resonate within my soul.

354. Stillness

We can make our minds so like still water
That beings gather about us.
— William Butler Yeats

We move too fast these days. And too loudly. Although humans were not originally made to go faster than a few miles an hour, we were born with the capacity to modify ourselves. We have added wings and wheels, so we can go faster than the original bipedal model. There is a cost, though. When we go faster, speed takes its toll, on both body and soul. The jet lag that one often feels after flying can be understood as the soul trying to catch up with the body, which has been rapidly and miraculously transported miles away by an airplane. Even in the woods, modern men often move rapidly about in that frenetic industrial pace, as if we were machines.

When we slow down, our emotions can catch up with us, emerging to guide our pace. The emotions vary; when a man is guided by his emotions, his pace varies. Within still water there is much life. As we look within we can perceive much.

Today I will slow down. Quiet down and see how I feel and think differently. I may need to go somewhere special, perhaps into a meadow or beneath a tree. As I silence my mind, what moves toward me? What do I perceive? What is at my center?

355. Self-Love

For what is man? Man is his heart. A dead heart means a dead man; a living heart a living man.

—Hazrat Inayat Khan

The first time I said, "I love myself," a deep sense of shame welled up inside me. I remember laughing to cover the deep embarrassment I felt. When the person I was with asked me why I laughed, I answered, "I felt funny." I laughed again, trying to shrug off my feelings, but I could not. As I focused on what I was feeling, my shame turned into deep grief, and I experienced the frightened little boy I once was.

As I cried and grieved for that lonely, abused little boy, I began to really feel that I *could* love myself. It was painful to turn inward and experience what had been locked inside for so long. But in order to truly love myself, I had to first love *all* of me, especially that scared little boy who felt so ashamed. The journey to wholeness can begin with a simple statement of self-love.

Today I will practice saying, "I love myself."

356. Darkness

If I reached my hands down, near the earth,
I could take handfuls of darkness!
A darkness was always there, which we
never noticed.

—Robert Bly

Today is the winter solstice, the longest night of the year—the most darkness. From this time on the light will increase. That darkness is always there, even when we ignore it. Its gifts are substantial. Under its cover much that is creative has been and can be done.

Many of us fear the dark. We fear the unknown, the confusion, and the chaos that darkness represents. Yet from these fertile forces much can grow. The night is full of activity—our dancing dreams and the bustling of nocturnal animals, who can help prepare the day.

In the darkness vision does not disappear; it is merely different. You can improve your night vision and night learning by bringing attention to them. Certain things that are always there, such as stars, become visible at night. In outer darkness an inner light can emerge. Before there was light, darkness existed, and after the light of life flickers out there will be more darkness, life's eternal context.

Today I will remember a time when I enjoyed a particular night. I may try to find a place away from city lights where I can see the stars. I will absorb their light and reflect on whatever meaning they may have for me on this darkest of nights.

357. Sacred Space

When I would recreate myself, I seek the darkest wood . . . the most dismal swamp. I enter the swamp as a sacred space. . . . There is the strength.

—Henry David Thoreau

Sacred space is where the transcendent, holy, and divine can appear. There are many places that become sacred because of what happens there or through the intention of those who gather. A church can be sacred, and so can a grove of trees. For some people an eating table is sacred. A couple's bed can be sacred. A men's lodge is a sacred space. One's work space can be sacred, especially if it is approached and entered with a sacred attitude. A sacred space points beyond itself, to a higher meaning. When one enters that space he feels its difference from other space immediately.

Sacred spaces have boundaries, which are important to respect. When those boundaries are violated, the space is endangered. Protecting boundaries is essential, as is expanding them at times to be more inclusive. Earth-loving peoples have a keen sense of sacred space. This sense is one of the many contributions of indigenous people to modern people.

Today I will go to a sacred space, one that is familiar to me or that I discover for the first time. I will go without much expectation concerning what might happen. I will just be there.

358. Soul

. . . my soul is a dark forest.
. . . my known self will never be more than
a little clearing in the forest.
. . . gods, strange gods, come forth from the
forest
into the clearing of my known self, and then
go back.

—D. H. Lawrence

To D. H. Lawrence, the soul is "a dark forest"—something unknown, hidden, only partially clear. He contrasts his soul with his "known self," which is how the soul manifests itself when there is a "clearing." The aspects of his soul that manifest in the self he calls "gods, strange gods." By this term he implies that the soul has powers that lie beyond one's capacity to fully understand rationally.

How much we know, how little we know. Do you really know why you do what you do? Perhaps the soul is guiding you. We can understand the soul as a perspective on things, a guiding intelligence. The soul is what is essential. Each soul is unique, particular. Souls have motion in them, connecting us to ideas, places, people.

Today I will make a clearing in my known self to allow my soul to manifest there. Toward what does my soul guide me? What does my soul desire?

359. Music

Without music life would be a mistake.
          —Friedrich Nietzsche

Music has the power to evoke images and feelings. Life music has more capacity to move us than recorded music. If you do not already make your own music, you may want to consider doing so.

Every man's soul makes a musical sound; for Francis of Assisi it was a stringed instrument, and for Thoreau the flute. For many contemporary men, the heartbeat of the drum has come to have special meaning. Music is a gift from the Divine. It can dramatically change how we are feeling.

Today I will release myself to music. I can find some music that speaks to me, opens me up, calls up images.

360. The Child

Give me back
the soul I had as a child,
matured by fairy tales,
with its hat of feathers
and its wooden sword.
—Federico García Lorca

Let's celebrate the child and his birth today. By honoring the child, the one within as well as the one in the outer world, we celebrate innocence, beginning, and the unity of all. As we grow, we individuate and differentiate; these are basically healthy processes. But we often lose touch with the child's connection to all that is, including other people, animals, and plants. The child offers us the gift of imagination. When a man loses contact with his imagination, he loses his child; part of him goes dead. The child represents vitality, ingenuity, and a sense of flair; without these a man becomes boring.

The soul we have now, as adults, differs from the soul we had as children. We make our souls; they are not static. They grow. But they can also be damaged, wounded, and diminished. Soul-making is a process that can be encouraged through various art forms, support groups, and in other ways. Making contact with one's Inner Divine Child can reinvigorate a man.

As a man matures, he will benefit if his pilgrimage includes rediscovering the child's awe and wonder in the face of emerging life.

How is your child today? What does he need? From what might he benefit? How can you care for and nurture him? Might he like you to wrestle with him? Or hold him?

361. Absent Fathers

DECEMBER 26

Fit out a ship with twenty oars, the best you
can come by,
and go out to ask about your father, who is
long absent.

—Homer

Fathers remain too often absent, gone even more now than they were before. The absence of fathers is epidemic in our society —fathers physically, emotionally, or otherwise gone. Children's longing and hunger for their fathers often results.

Father hunger can stimulate a man to go on a search, which may lead him to other men. Or this hunger can open up into a deep wound and be projected, unconsciously, on to other men, especially older men, perhaps causing some damage. Healing from father wounds is essential to relating to other men, as well as to women. Failing to resolve issues with our fathers can inhibit our capacity to get close to and trust other men.

When our father is absent, we have two main options for dealing with the wound: ignore it and pass it on to our children or to others from whom we withhold, or tend to the wound and mend it. Such effort is known as recovery. Some of the work on absent fathers can be done directly with one's own father, alive or dead. Such work can also be done indirectly at men's gatherings or in ongoing groups.

Was my father absent? Or partly absent? What did I miss from him? How might I get today what I did not get then? Is there a man in my life who could be helpful?

362. Patterns

Love that which is woven for you in the pattern of your destiny. What could be better suited for your growth?

—Marcus Aurelius

Flying over fields, we notice their patterns, how well organized they are. Nature is full of patterns, only some of which we recognize. All kinds of patterns exist—life patterns, relationship patterns, agricultural patterns, cloud patterns, trees.

Men, too, are full of patterns, only some of which we understand. Discerning our own patterns and those of our loved ones can be helpful. If we figure out a pattern, then we may be able to predict what will come next—in our lives or in the life of someone to whom we are close. We can perceive how things are connected and how they are unfolding.

Today I will try to see beyond my own ego to discover the larger pattern—which some call the Divine Will—of which I am a part. I will explore the fabric within which I and my brothers are threads.

363. One Day at a Time

The nicest thing about the future is that it comes one day at a time.

—Anonymous

It really doesn't help to worry about the future. That worry is simply a sign that I've lost my perspective, and that I need to take better care of myself. If I do the things that nurture me, if I show up for my life one day at a time, the future will unfold naturally. This does not mean I will not face challenges or disappointments: every day is full of surprises. It means instead that, being fully available for each moment, I embrace what is—now—rather than spend this precious time in worry and fear. When I live in today, the challenges and surprises do not overwhelm me.

When I find myself living in the wreckage of the future, I will focus on what I can do right *now to nurture myself.*

364. Finding Treasure in the Dark

In a dark time, the eye begins to see.
—Theodore Roethke

Sometimes a man must sit alone in darkness for a while in order to remember how to feel. He waits for the pain to move through him, to make its own kind of sense. He waits for his wonder at life to return.

Many of us have feared these dark times, but life keeps providing them just the same: the death of a dad, a divorce, a friend's departure. To enter these places in ourselves, we seek solitude. There we call on the love we have felt for a wife, a lover, for God, for a child, or for someone now lost. Rekindling the memory of that love within is like finding buried gold. Its pure power lights our path out of the darkness, and we value it as our greatest treasure.

The light a man discovers in a dark time is the light that will warm him again later, when the sun is hidden or when his own death draws near. If discovered, cherished, and allowed to expand, such light makes every darkness bearable, every breath a cause for celebration, and every love enduring.

Today I'll look for that magnificent light shining within me, the light that shows itself also in the dark times. Today I'll give myself solitude and time to contemplate.

365. Restrictions

For everything there is a season and a time for every matter under heaven.

—Ecclesiastes 3:1

Winter can bring restrictions, especially in cold areas. Travel can be more difficult. We may have to stay inside and at home more. As hibernating animals show us, such natural restrictions can induce a pause that is followed by growth and creativity. Humans also seem to have seasonal cycles; contemporary men seem to respect these cycles less than did the ancients.

Winter can be a time to rest, renew, and restore ourselves, with the anticipation that spring will bring a different kind of energy. Winter is a good time for prayer, meditation, and inspirational reading. Going inside, we can prepare for coming back out. Restrictions enable the creative person to shift gears and manifest his energy in another way. What appears at first to be problematic can be seen as a gift. Unable to do one thing, we can expand our awareness and do something else.

How do I feel restricted today? How might that be a gift? How can I shift my focus from being deprived by the restriction to being opened to something else?

366. Growing New

Even at the age of seventy or eighty, as long as you still have one breath in you, restoration is possible.

—Liu I-ming

Recovery is not a respecter of age. The young man and the elder have many of the same opportunities to heal their inner wounds, to turn their backs on pain and loneliness, to face a new direction and follow a truer path.

Some men think they are "too old" to begin again. But there are seventy-five-year-old men who have wept bitter tears for the fathers they wanted and never had, who grieved over the thousands of dollars spent on thousands of bottles of booze to anesthetize their pain, only to end up alienating themselves from life and family. There are elders who, at long last, were able to weep for lost childhoods.

But as these men mourn their losses, the light in their eyes becomes brighter. They cast off the burden of decades of grief and stand taller. In such moments the aging process reverses itself. The moment we throw off our pain and fear, we come closest to what is Divine in us. Nor is this some vague inner change; the light of freedom shines in the face.

Today I'll grow new, trusting that it's never too late to heal.

Acknowledgments

I would like to acknowledge my two coauthors for their contribution to this work. When I first conceived writing a men's meditation book, I knew I did not want to write it alone. My next thought was that I wanted to work on this project with my friend John. After some discussion, he and I decided to ask Shepherd to join us. Shepherd agreed, and we were off and running. What an experience! I have never worked on a writing project with two men before, and the process was exhilarating, frustrating, and humbling. I learned a lot about myself and about teamwork during the two years we worked on this book. My gift from this project has been the deepening of my friendship with John and my new friendship with Shepherd. Thanks, guys.

An acknowledgment is never complete without naming the unsung heroes who make a book really happen. My wife and life partner, Ceci Miller-Kritsberg, edited the first draft of my meditations, and her loving support and guidance were invaluable. It would be impossible to name all of the men and women who have nurtured, supported, and encouraged me during my life and who have been my mentors and spiritual guides. To this small army of people, as well as the loving guidance of a Higher Power, I extend my heartfelt thanks.

W.K.

This book would not have been written were it not for the men who have

367

loved me, worked with me, supported me, and cared for me. My special thanks to all the men who have attended my workshops and men's gatherings—you have taught me a great deal, more than you might suspect. Also I want to thank the men who were, and who are now, in my men's groups—more than you might know, your consistency and determination has healed me.

I especially want to thank my dear friend Wayne for inviting me into this project, and my life-long buddy, Shepherd, for hanging in there. They worked with me to bring not only a wealth of creativity to the book but to teach me a lot about collaborating, partnering, paying attention to detail, and sparring without getting hurt. And of course I want to thank the other truly generous men with whom I partner: Dan Jones, Robert Bly, Robert Moore, and Bill Stott. These men touch my life in a way that words cannot express.

Ceci Miller-Kritsberg's guidance, encouragement, editing, and friendship improved the project immeasurably.

Writing this book—like the trees, rain, rivers, mountains, animals, and plants and the beautiful people who've come and gone, come and stayed—has taught me, healed me, and helped me. To those who have gone on down the road: know you are not forgotten. To those who have stayed—my partner, Bev, and her daughter, Kate, and others: know that you are loved.

J.L.

Place is important. I began my part of this book in Berkeley, California, in 1991. Then I moved to a farm in the rolling hills of Sonoma County on the northern California coast and began working the land

and living within its groves of tall redwoods and old oaks. The splendid high desert in northern New Mexico and the fertile Findhorn Foundation in Scotland provided meditative places for my writing to unfold. Thanks to these sacred places and the animals, plants, and people who live there for their stimulation and support.

The Kokopelli Traveling Men's Lodge, which I direct in its men's, gender, and soul work around the world, has inspired me. I hear the words of my Lodge brothers as I write—including the elder Doug von Koss, Joe Roberts and Ross LewAllen of Santa Fe, artist Larry Stefl, and fireman Ray Gatchalian. The Sons of Orpheus, which I helped found in 1986 and whose nearly forty men still go strong without me, has provided an important container for my development, thanks to men like Bruce Silverman, Dan Zola, and Jay Roller. My new friends from Sonoma County, including Russell Sutter and Robert Leverant, and members of the Redwood Men's Center, especially Don Morris and Larry Robinson, have added their wisdom to my writing.

Of my many teachers, Robert Bly stands out. I met him twenty-five years ago as a young officer in the U.S. Army, and he has been a good sparring partner. To those men who nourished my development in the men's movement in the 1970s, especially Joseph Pleck, and in the 1980s, including the Rev. Rob McCann, I extend my appreciation. To the hundreds of men with whom I have been in men's groups, and to the thousands with whom I have been at men's gatherings, I thank you.

I also appreciate the women who are starting to join us in the growing gender reconciliation movement. Members of other cultures—including Elena Avila, Allan Chinen, Gilberto Madrid, and Roberto Almanzan—have given me special insight into masculine diversity. Other key teachers include my farming Uncle Dale, Nelle Morton, May Sarton, and Jean Shinoda Bolen. The work of two Buddhists has contributed significantly to this book: the wonderful poet and translator Stephen Mitchell, and the gifted teacher Jack Kornfield.

With my coauthors I have experienced the range of feelings and actions that characterize real relationships: love and frustration, pulling back and going ahead, clarity and doubt, and precious moments of intimacy. May my friendship and work with Wayne and John continue.

My contribution would not have been possible without the women in my life, especially Arlene Otani, who brings a richness from her Buddhist practice to everything she does.

S.B.

Thanks to our editors at Bantam: Leslie Meredith, Linda Lowenstein, Paula Dunham, Terry E. D. Moore, editorial assistant Alison Rivers, and especially to Toni Burbank, who maintained a clear vision of this work during the times when ours faltered. Ron Schaumburg's editing skill, careful attention to detail, and deep understanding of the material was essential in tying the material together into a cohesive whole.

W.K., J.L., S.B.

Credits

By Wayne Kritsberg:
Jan. 1, 3, 5, 8, 11, 15, 17, 19, 25–26, 29–30;
Feb. 3, 5, 8, 10, 16–17, 19, 23, 28; Mar. 1–
2, 6, 12, 16–17, 20–23, 27–28; Apr. 3–5, 12,
16, 18, 22, 24, 27, 29; May 2, 8, 12, 16, 22–
24, 26, 29, 31; Jun. 7–20, 24–25, 28–29;
Jul. 4, 6, 10, 25–28; Aug. 17–18, 24, 26–27,
30–31; Sep. 3, 13–14, 20, 26–27, 30; Oct. 5,
8–11, 14, 17, 19, 25, 30; Nov. 11, 13–14,
18, 21–22, 26; Dec. 2, 6–8, 10–14, 20, 28.

By John Lee:
Jan. 2, 7, 10, 14, 16, 20–21, 27–28; Feb. 4,
6–7, 11–12, 21, 24, 26; Mar. 3–4, 7, 9, 11,
18–19, 25, 29–30; Apr. 7–9, 11, 15, 17, 21,
25, 28; May 1, 7, 9, 11, 15, 17–18, 21, 25,
27–28; Jun. 1; Jul. 1, 3, 8–9, 12, 15, 17–19;
21–24, 29–30; Aug. 1–4, 7–9, 12–15, 21–22,
28; Sep. 1, 4, 6, 8–11, 19, 24–25, 28;
Oct. 1–2, 13, 20–24, 26, 28; Nov. 1, 4–6, 9–
10, 15–16, 19–20, 23, 28; Dec. 9, 29, 31.

By Shepherd Bliss:
Jan. 4, 6, 9, 12–13, 18, 22–24, 31; Feb. 1–2,
9, 13–15, 18, 20, 22, 25, 27, 29; Mar. 5, 8,
10, 13–15, 24, 26, 31; Apr. 1–2, 6, 10, 13–
14, 19–20, 23, 26, 30; May 3–6, 10, 13–14,
19–20, 30; Jun. 2–6, 21–23, 26–27, 30;
Jul. 2, 5, 7, 11, 13–14, 16, 20, 31; Aug. 5–6,
10–11, 16, 19–20, 23, 25, 29; Sep. 2, 5, 7,
12, 15–18, 21–23, 29; Oct. 3–4, 6–7, 12, 15–
16, 18, 27, 29, 31; Nov. 2–3, 7–8, 12, 17,
24–25, 27, 29–30; Dec. 1, 3–5, 15–19, 21–
27, 30.

Index

About the Authors

WAYNE KRITSBERG, M.A., one of the founders of the modern recovery movement, is internationally recognized for his innovative work with adult survivors of childhood trauma. A therapist, author, and lecturer, Wayne facilitates counselor training and personal recovery workshops throughout the international community.

Wayne's other books include *The Invisible Wound: A New Approach to Healing Childhood Sexual Trauma; The Adult Children of Alcoholics Syndrome; From Discovery to Recovery; Gifts: Advanced Skills for Alcoholism Counselors' Gifts for Personal Growth and Recovery;* and *Healing Together: A Guide to Intimacy and Recovery for Codependent Couples.* Wayne is the author of two popular booklets, "Chronic Shock and Adult Children of Alcoholics" and "Am I in a Codependent Relationship?"

Wayne has studied eastern mysticism and western psychology for more than twenty-five years, and is a longtime meditator. He consciously endeavors to weave these disciplines throughout his professional and personal life. Now in his fifties, Wayne's personal focus is on family intimacy, fathering, and environmental concerns. He is deeply involved in exploring midlife spirituality and in advocating for healthier and more environmentally sound lifestyle choices. Wayne lives with his family in Olympia, Washington, where he has a private therapy practice and leads midlife workshops and retreats.

While it is not always possible for Wayne to answer all the mail he receives from readers, he appreciates learning about their experiences. To share your experience, write him at 2103 Harrison Northwest, Suite 2163, Olympia, Washington 98502. To obtain a catalog of audiotapes and books by Wayne Kritsberg, to place an order, or to find out about his workshops and retreats, write to the above address or call (206) 754-2106.

JOHN LEE is the author of the best-selling books *The Flying Boy: Healing the Wounded Man; Flying Boy II; At My Father's Wedding; Facing the Fire: Experiencing and Expressing Anger Appropriately;* and *Writing from the Body.* In addition, he has released a series of audiotapes on relationships, including *Nobody at Home: Looking at Hidden Addictions; Beyond Jung;* and *Grieving—A Key to Healing.*

He is internationally recognized as a leader in the personal growth, men's, and recovery movements. Founder of the Austin Men's Center, John gives workshops and lectures on issues concerning men, adult children from dysfunctional families, and relationships. He trains therapists internationally in a program called Primary Emotional Energy Recover (PEER), which he founded with partner Dan Jones.

A frequent featured guest on such programs as *Oprah Winfrey, Sally Jessy Raphael,* and others, John has been the subject of articles in *The New York Times, Changes* magazine, and *Newsweek.* He has taught World Religions and Literature at the University of Alabama, the University of Texas, and Austin Community College.

He lives in Austin, Texas, with his partner, Beverly Barnes, and her daughter, Kate Montgomery.

For more information about publications, tapes, workshops, and speaking engagements, write John Lee, West Austin Station, PO Box 5892, Austin, Texas 78763, or call (512) 445-7992.

SHEPHERD BLISS, D. MIN., a pioneer in the men's movement since the 1970s, was the first to apply the term *mythopoetic* to this work. Having earned a doctorate in ministry at the University of Chicago Divinity School, he completed postdoctoral study at Harvard University, where he served as a counselor for a decade. For a dozen years he taught Men's Studies at John F. Kennedy University.

Dr. Bliss has served as a Methodist minister and was a U.S. Army officer during the Vietnam era. He has been active for many years in movements for peace, deep ecology, and gender reconciliation, and for four years led an Episcopal church men's program. Currently he directs the Kokopelli Traveling Men's Lodge, which tours the U.S., Canada, and Europe featuring ceremonial artists and musicians who present stories, lectures, music, and poetry at gatherings and rituals.

An award-winning speaker, Dr. Bliss has hosted his own radio program and is a frequent guest on talk shows, including *Oprah Winfrey* and *Donahue.* He published hundreds of articles in men's movement, spiritual, and alternative publications; has contributed essays to over a dozen books, including *Boyhood: Growing Up Male; To Be a Man; Wingspan: Inside the Men's Movement; Men and Intimacy; New Men, New Minds;* and *The Best Man;* and is editor of *The New Holistic Health Handbook.* Currently approaching his fiftieth year, he farms a few acres outside Sebastopol, California.

Shepherd Bliss writes and edits The Men's, Gender, and Soul Newsletter, *which includes information on events and resources. For a free copy write: PO Box 1040, Sebastopol, California 95473, or call (707) 829-8185.*